D1335281

GOLF RULES
illustrated

SIXTH EDITION
PUBLISHED JUNE 1988

COMPILED BY

THE ROYAL AND ANCIENT GOLF CLUB
OF ST ANDREWS

ILLUSTRATIONS BY PETER DAVIDSON

HAMLYN

Foreword

Successive Rules Committees of the Royal and Ancient Golf Club of St. Andrews and the United States Golf Association have tried to simplify the Rules of Golf but, because of the multitude of situations which can and do arise in the course of a round, and the differing climatic and geographical conditions under which the game is played, this is not an easy task. Consequently, the Rules are in some areas complicated.

Many of us in conducting teaching sessions on the Rules have found the value of photographs and diagrams in explaining points on which our audience may have been uncertain, and we believe that Golf Rules Illustrated serves a similar purpose.

In this Sixth Edition we have sought to include illustrations covering (a) those items which are most frequently the subject of questions (b) changes in the Rules which became effective on 1 January 1988, and (c) new and revised Decisions which have been made since the last Edition of Golf Rules Illustrated was published.

I hope that this book will be of assistance and will stimulate what we believe is a growing interest among players throughout the world in the Rules of the game.

W.J.F Bryce

W.J.F. BRYCE, Chairman
Rules of Golf Committee,
Royal and Ancient Golf Club of St. Andrews.

This edition published in 1989 by
The Hamlyn Publishing Group Limited,
a division of the Octopus Publishing Group,
Michelin House, 81 Fulham Road, London SW3 6RB,
and distributed for them by
Octopus Distribution Services Limited,
Rushden, Northamptonshire NN10 9RZ

© 1969, 1972, 1976, 1980, 1985, 1988
The Royal and Ancient Golf Club of St Andrews
and IPC Publications

ISBN 0 600 566 242
Printed in the United Kingdom

The Rules of Golf which are printed are
copyright © of the Royal and Ancient Golf Club of St Andrews
and the United States Golf Association.

All rights reserved. This book, or parts thereof,
may not be reproduced without the written permission
of the Royal and Ancient Golf Club of St Andrews.

GOLF RULES
illustrated

CONTENTS

Section I Etiquette

Courtesy on the Course

Safety

Prior to playing a stroke or making a practice swing, the player should ensure that no one is standing close by or in a position to be hit by the club, the ball or any stones, pebbles, twigs or the like which may be moved by the stroke or swing.

Consideration for Other Players

The player who has the honour should be allowed to play before his opponent or fellow-competitor tees his ball.

No one should move, talk or stand close to or directly behind the ball or the hole when a player is addressing the ball or making a stroke.

In the interest of all, players should play without delay.

No player should play until the players in front are out of range. Players searching for a ball should signal the players behind them to pass as soon as it becomes apparent that the ball will not easily be found. They should not search for five minutes before doing so. They should not continue play until the players following them have passed and are out of range.

When the play of a hole has been completed, players should immediately leave the putting green.

That pebble nearly hit me. Before you take a practice swing you should always be sure that no one is standing in such a position that he could be hit by anything you dislodge like a stone, a pebble or a twig.

We're holding up that group behind and we've lost more than a hole on the people in front. I suggest we should invite them to play through.

Priority on the Course

In the absence of special rules, two-ball matches should have precedence over and be entitled to pass any three- or four-ball match.

A single player has no standing and should give way to a match of any kind.

Any match playing a whole round is entitled to pass a match playing a shorter round.

If a match fails to keep its place on the course and loses more than one clear hole on the players in front, it should invite the match following to pass.

Holes in Bunkers

Before leaving a bunker, a player should carefully fill up and smooth over all holes and footprints made by him.

Replace Divots; Repair Ball-Marks and Damage by Spikes

Through the green, a player should ensure that any turf cut or displaced by him is replaced at once and pressed down and that any damage to the putting green made by a ball is carefully repaired. Damage to the putting green caused by golf shoe spikes should be repaired *on completion of the hole.*

Damage to Greens – Flagsticks, Bags, etc.

Players should ensure that, when putting down bags or the flagstick, no damage is done to the putting green and that neither they nor their caddies damage the hole by standing close to it, in handling the flagstick or in removing the ball from the hole. The flagstick should be properly replaced in the hole before the players leave the putting green. Players should not damage the putting green by leaning on their putters, particularly when removing the ball from the hole.

Golf Carts

Local notices regulating the movement of golf carts should be strictly observed.

Damage Through Practice Swings

In taking practice swings, players should avoid causing damage to the course, particularly the tees, by removing divots.

Always repair divots. This is part of looking after the course (top right). Always repair carefully ball marks on the putting green (above). Don't lean on your putter when you are removing the ball from the hole (bottom right).

Section II Definitions

Addressing the Ball

A player has "addressed the ball" when he has taken his <u>stance</u> and has also grounded his club, except that in a <u>hazard</u> a player has addressed the ball when he has taken his stance.

The player is deliberately refraining from grounding his club, i.e. from "addressing" the ball. If he grounded his club, and the wind then moved the ball, he would incur a penalty stroke.

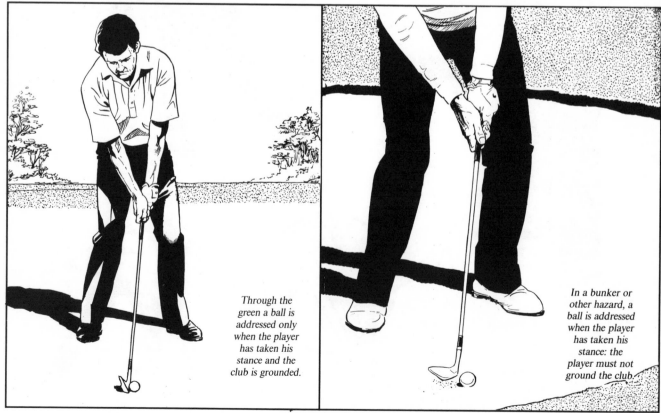

Through the green a ball is addressed only when the player has taken his stance and the club is grounded.

In a bunker or other hazard, a ball is addressed when the player has taken his stance: the player must not ground the club.

Advice

"Advice" is any counsel or suggestion which could influence a player in determining his play, the choice of a club or the method of making a stroke.

Information on the Rules or on matters of public information, such as the position of hazards or the flagstick on the putting green, is not advice.

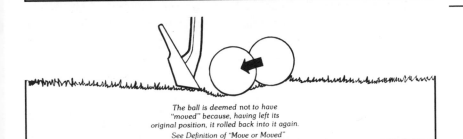

*The ball is deemed not to have "moved" because, having left its original position, it rolled back into it again.
See Definition of "Move or Moved"*

Ball Deemed to Move
See "Move or Moved".

Ball Holed
See "Holed".

Ball Lost
See "Lost Ball".

Ball in Play

A ball is "in play" as soon as the player has made a stroke on the teeing ground. It remains in play until holed out, except when it is lost, out of bounds or lifted, or another ball has been substituted under an applicable Rule, whether or not such Rule permits substitution; a ball so substituted becomes the ball in play.

Bunker

A "bunker" is a hazard consisting of a prepared area of ground, often a hollow, from which turf or soil has been removed and replaced with sand or the like. Grass-covered ground bordering or within a bunker is not part of the bunker. The margin of a bunker extends vertically downwards, but not upwards.

My ball is well down in that rabbit hole. Since the margin of the bunker extends vertically downwards my ball is not in the bunker so when I take relief I do not have to drop in the bunker.

Caddie

A "caddie" is one who carries or handles a player's clubs during play and otherwise assists him in accordance with the Rules.

When one caddie is employed by more than one player, he is always deemed to be the caddie of the player whose ball is involved, and equipment carried by him is deemed to be that player's equipment, except when the caddie acts upon specific directions of another player, in which case he is considered to be that other player's caddie.

Casual Water

"Casual water" is any temporary accumulation of water on the course which is visible before or after the player takes his stance and is not in a water hazard. Snow and ice are either casual water or loose impediments, at the option of the player, except that manufactured ice is an obstruction. Dew is not casual water.

Committee

The "Committee" is the committee in charge of the competition or, if the matter does not arise in a competition, the committee in charge of the course.

Competitor

A "competitor" is a player in a stroke competition. A "fellow-competitor" is any person with whom the competitor plays. Neither is partner of the other.

In stroke play foursome and four-ball competitions, where the context so admits, the word "competitor" or "fellow-competitor" includes his partner.

Course

The "course" is the whole area within which play is permitted (see Rule 33-2).

Equipment

"Equipment" is anything used, worn or carried by or for the player except any ball he has played at the hole being played and any small object, such as a coin or a tee, when used to mark the position of a ball or the extent of an area in which a ball is to be dropped. Equipment includes a golf cart, whether or not motorised. If such a cart is shared by more than one player, its status under the Rules is the same as that of a caddie employed by more than one player. See "Caddie".

Fellow-Competitor
See "Competitor".

Flagstick

The "flagstick" is a movable straight indicator, with or without bunting or other material attached, centred in the hole to show its position. It shall be circular in cross-section.

Forecaddie

A "forecaddie" is one who is employed by the Committee to indicate to players the position of balls during play. He is an outside agency.

Ground Under Repair

"Ground under repair" is any portion of the course so marked by order of the Committee or so declared by its authorised representative. It includes material piled for removal and a hole made by a greenkeeper, even if not so marked. Stakes and lines defining ground under repair are in such ground. The margin of ground under repair extends vertically downwards, but not upwards.

Note 1: Grass cuttings and other material left on the course which have been abandoned and are not intended to be removed are not ground under repair unless so marked.

Note 2: The Committee may make a Local Rule prohibiting play from ground under repair.

Hazards

A "hazard" is any bunker or water hazard.

Hole

The "hole" shall be 4¼ inches (108 mm) in diameter and at least 4 inches (100 mm) deep. If a lining is used, it shall be sunk at least 1 inch (25 mm) below the putting green surface unless the nature of the soil makes it impracticable to do so; its outer diameter shall not exceed 4¼ inches (108 mm).

Holed

A ball is "holed" when it is at rest within the circumference of the hole and all of it is below the level of the lip of the hole.

Honour

The side entitled to play first from the teeing ground is said to have the "honour".

Lateral Water Hazard

A "lateral water hazard" is a water hazard or that part of a water hazard so situated that it is not possible or is deemed by the Committee to be impracticable to drop a ball behind the water hazard in accordance with Rule 26-1b.

That part of a water hazard to be played as a lateral water hazard should be distinctively marked.

Note: Lateral water hazards should be defined by red stakes or lines.

Loose Impediments

"Loose impediments" are natural objects such as stones, leaves, twigs, branches and the like, dung, worms and insects and casts or heaps made by them, provided they are not fixed or growing, are not solidly embedded and do not adhere to the ball.

Sand and loose soil are loose impediments on the putting green, but not elsewhere.

Snow and ice are either casual water or loose impediments, at the option of the player, except that manufactured ice is an obstruction.

Dew is not a loose impediment.

Lost Ball

A ball is "lost" if:

a. It is not found or identified as his by the player within five-minutes after the player's side or his or their caddies have begun to search for it; or

b. The player has put another ball into play under the Rules, even though he may not have searched for the original ball; or

c. The player has played any stroke with a provisional ball from the place where the original ball is likely to be or from a point nearer the hole than that place, whereupon the provisional ball becomes the ball in play.

Time spent in playing a wrong ball is not counted in the five minute period allowed for search.

Marker

A "marker" is one who is appointed by the Committee to record a competitor's score in stroke play. He may be a fellow-competitor. He is not a referee.

Matches

See "Sides and Matches".

Move or Moved

A ball is deemed to have "moved" if it leaves its position and comes to rest in any other place.

Observer

An "observer" is one who is appointed by the Committee to assist a referee to decide questions of fact and to report to him any breach of a Rule. An observer should not attend the flagstick, stand at or mark the position of the hole, or lift the ball or mark its position.

Obstructions

An "obstruction" is anything artificial, including the artificial surfaces and sides of roads and paths and manufactured ice, except:

a. Objects defining out of bounds, such as walls, fences, stakes and railings;

b. Any part of an immovable artificial object which is out of bounds; and

c. Any construction declared by the Committee to be an integral part of the course.

Out of Bounds

"Out of bounds" is ground on which play is prohibited.

When out of bounds is defined by reference to stakes or a fence or as being beyond stakes or a fence, the out of bounds line is determined by the nearest inside points of the stakes or fence posts at ground level excluding angled supports.

When out of bounds is defined by a line on the ground, the line itself is out of bounds.

The out of bounds line extends vertically upwards and downwards.

A ball is out of bounds when all of it lies out of bounds.

A player may stand out of bounds to play a ball lying within bounds.

Outside Agency

An "outside agency" is any agency not part of the match or, in stroke play, not part of a competitor's side, and includes a referee, a marker, an observer or a forecaddie.

Neither wind nor water is an outside agency.

Partner

A "partner" is a player associated with another player on the same side.

In a threesome, foursome, best-ball or four-ball match, where the context so admits, the word "player" includes his partner or partners.

Penalty Stroke

A "penalty stroke" is one added to the score of a player or side under certain Rules. In a threesome or foursome, penalty strokes do not affect the order of play.

Provisional Ball

A "provisional ball" is a ball played under Rule 27-2 for a ball which may be lost outside a water hazard or may be out of bounds.

Putting Green

The "putting green" is all ground of the hole being played which is specially prepared for putting or otherwise defined as such by the Committee. A ball is on the putting green when any part of it touches the putting green.

Referee

A "referee" is one who is appointed by the Committee to accompany players to decide questions of fact and apply the Rules of Golf. He shall act on any breach of a Rule which he observes or is reported to him.

A referee should not attend the flagstick, stand at or mark the position of the hole, or lift the ball or mark its position.

DEFINITIONS

Rub of the Green

A "rub of the green" occurs when a ball in motion is accidentally deflected or stopped by any outside agency (see Rule 19-1).

Rule

The term "Rule" includes Local Rules made by the Committee under Rule 33-8a.

Sides and Matches

Side: A player, or two or more players who are partners.
Single: A match in which one plays against another.
Threesome: A match in which one plays against two, and each side plays one ball.
Foursome: A match in which two play against two, and each side plays one ball.
Three-ball: A match play competition in which three play against one another, each playing his own ball. Each player is playing two distinct matches.
Best-ball: A match in which one plays against the better ball of two or the best ball of three players.
Four-ball: A match in which two play their better ball against the better ball of two other players.

Stance

Taking the "stance" consists in a player placing his feet in position for and preparatory to making a stroke.

Stipulated Round

The "stipulated round" consists of playing the holes of the course in their correct sequence unless otherwise authorised by the Committee. The number of holes in a stipulated round is 18 unless a smaller number is authorised by the Committee. As to extension of stipulated round in match play, see Rule 2-3.

Stroke

A "stroke" is the forward movement of the club made with the intention of fairly striking at and moving the ball, but if a player checks his downswing voluntarily before the clubhead reaches the ball he is deemed not to have made a stroke.

Teeing Ground

The "teeing ground" is the starting place for the hole to be played. It is a rectangular area two club-lengths in depth, the front and the sides of which are defined by the outside limits of two tee-markers. A ball is outside the teeing ground when all of it lies outside the teeing ground.

Through the Green

"Through the green" is the whole area of the course except:
a. The teeing ground and putting green of the hole being played; and
b. All hazards on the course.

Water Hazard

A "water hazard" is any sea, lake, pond, river, ditch, surface drainage ditch or other open water course (whether or not containing water) and anything of a similar nature.
All ground or water within the margin of a water hazard is part of the water hazard. The margin of a water hazard extends vertically upwards and downwards. Stakes and lines defining the margins of water hazards are in the hazards.
Note: Water hazards (other than lateral water hazards) should be defined by yellow stakes or lines.

Wrong Ball

A "wrong ball" is any ball other than:
a. The ball in play,
b. A provisional ball or
c. In stroke play, a second ball played under Rule 3-3 or Rule 20-7b.
Note: Ball in play includes a ball substituted for the ball in play when the player is proceeding under an applicable Rule which does not permit substitution.

Section III The Rules of Play
THE GAME

RULE 1. The Game

Rule 1-1.
General

The Game of Golf consists in playing a ball from the teeing ground into the hole by a stroke or successive strokes in accordance with the Rules.

Rule 1-2.
Exerting Influence on Ball

No player or caddie shall take any action to influence the position or the movement of a ball except in accordance with the Rules.

PENALTY FOR BREACH OF RULE 1-2:
Match Play — Loss of hole; Stroke play — Two strokes.
Note: In the case of a serious breach of Rule 1-2, the Committee may impose a penalty of disqualification.

I'd like to run this ball up with my putter. Can I mop up that water on the green with a towel?

No. You'd be influencing the movement of the ball.

Note. If the ball had been lying on the green, relief could have been taken by moving the ball under Rule 25-1b (iii) to avoid the casual water.

Rule 1-3.
Agreement to Waive Rules

Players shall not agree to exclude the operation of any Rule or to waive any penalty incurred.

PENALTY FOR BREACH OF RULE 1-3:
Match play — Disqualification of both sides;
Stroke play — Disqualification of competitors concerned.
(Agreeing to play out of turn in stroke play — see Rule 10-2c.)

I've just realised I've 15 clubs in my bag. I forgot to leave my spare putter in my locker. I declare it out of play and even though I won the 1st hole the match is all square.

That's nonsense! I don't play golf that way. I know the maximum 14 clubs Rule but I refuse to apply the penalty. You are one up, so let's carry on that way.

No — we must play by the Rules, otherwise we will both be disqualified for a breach of Rule 1-3.

If any point in dispute is not covered by the Rules, the decision shall be made in accordance with equity.

Rule 1-4.
Points Not Covered by Rules

RULE 2. Match Play

In match play the game is played by holes.
Except as otherwise provided in the Rules, a hole is won by the side which holes its ball in the fewer strokes. In a handicap match the lower net score wins the hole.
The reckoning of holes is kept by the terms: so many "holes up" or "all square", and so many "to play".
A side is "dormie" when it is as many holes up as there are holes remaining to be played.

Rule 2-1.
Winner of Hole; Reckoning of Holes

A hole is halved if each side holes out in the same number of strokes.
When a player has holed out and his opponent has been left with a stroke for the half, if the player thereafter incurs a penalty, the hole is halved.

Rule 2-2.
Halved Hole

Rule 2-3.
Winner of Match

A match (which consists of a stipulated round, unless otherwise decreed by the Committee) is won by the side which is leading by a number of holes greater than the number of holes remaining to be played.

The Committee may, for the purpose of settling a tie, extend the stipulated round to as many holes as are required for a match to be won.

Rule 2-4.
Concession of Next Stroke,
Hole or Match

When the opponent's ball is at rest or is deemed to be at rest under Rule 16-2, the player may concede the opponent to have holed out with his next stroke and the ball may be removed by either side with a club or otherwise.

A player may concede a hole or a match at any time prior to the conclusion of the hole or the match.

Concession of a stroke, hole or match may not be declined or withdrawn.

Rule 2-5.
Claims

In match play, if a doubt or dispute arises between the players and no duly authorised representative of the Committee is available within a reasonable time, the players shall continue the match without delay. Any claim, if it is to be considered by the Committee, must be made before any player in the match plays from the next teeing ground or, in the case of the last hole of the match, before all players in the match leave the putting green.

No later claim shall be considered unless it is based on facts previously unknown to the player making the claim and the player making the claim had been given wrong information (Rules 6-2a and 9) by an opponent. In any case, no later claim shall be considered after the result of the match has been officially announced, unless the Committee is satisfied that the opponent knew he was giving wrong information.

Rule 2-6.
General Penalty

The penalty for a breach of a Rule in match play is loss of hole except when otherwise provided.

RULE 3. Stroke Play

Rule 3-1.
Winner

The competitor who plays the stipulated round or rounds in the fewest strokes is the winner.

Rule 3-2.
Failure to Hole Out

If a competitor fails to hole out at any hole and does not correct his mistake before he plays a stroke from the next teeing ground or, in the case of the last hole of the round, before he leaves the putting green, *he shall be disqualified.*

Rule 3-3.
Doubt as to Procedure

a. Procedure

In stroke play only, when during play of a hole a competitor is doubtful of his rights or procedure, he may, without penalty, play a second ball. After the situation which caused the doubt has arisen, the competitor should, before taking further action, announce to his marker or a fellow-competitor his decision to invoke this Rule and the ball with which he will score if the Rules permit.

The competitor shall report the facts to the Committee before returning his score card unless he scores the same with both balls; if he fails to do so, *he shall be disqualified.*

b. Determination of Score for Hole

If the Rules allow the procedure selected in advance by the competitor, the score with the ball selected shall be his score for the hole.

If the competitor fails to announce in advance his decision to invoke this Rule or his selection, the score with the original ball or, if the original ball is not one of the balls being played, the first ball put into play shall count if the Rules allow the procedure adopted for such ball.

Note: A second ball played under Rule 3-3 is not a provisional ball under Rule 27-2.

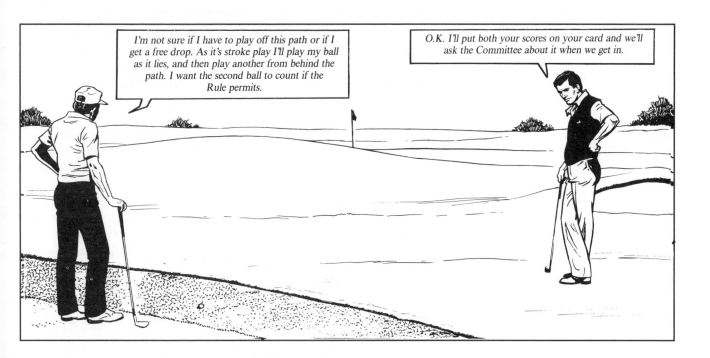

Rule 3-4.
Refusal to Comply with a Rule

If a competitor refuses to comply with a Rule affecting the rights of another competitor, *he shall be disqualified.*

Rule 3-5.
General Penalty

The penalty for a breach of a Rule in stroke play is two strokes except when otherwise provided.

CLUBS AND THE BALL

> The Royal and Ancient Golf Club of St. Andrews and the United States Golf Association reserve the right to change the Rules and make and change the interpretations relating to clubs, balls and other implements at any time.

RULE 4. CLUBS

> If there may be any reasonable basis for doubt as to whether a club which is to be manufactured conforms with Rule 4 and Appendix II, the manufacturer should submit a sample to the Royal and Ancient Golf Club of St. Andrews for a ruling, such sample to become its property for reference purposes. If a manufacturer fails to do so, he assumes the risk of a ruling that the club does not conform with the Rules of Golf.
>
> A player in doubt as to the conformity of a club should consult the Royal and Ancient Golf Club of St. Andrews.

Rule 4-1.
Form and Make of Clubs

A club is an implement designed to be used for striking the ball. A putter is a club designed primarily for use on the putting green. The player's clubs shall conform with the provisions of this Rule and with the specifications and interpretations set forth in Appendix II.

a. General The club shall be composed of a shaft and a head. All parts of the club shall be fixed so that the club is one unit. The club shall not be designed to be adjustable except for weight. The club shall not be substantially different from the traditional and customary form and make.

b. Shaft The shaft shall be generally straight, with the same bending and twisting properties in any direction, and shall be attached to the clubhead at the heel either directly or through a single plain neck or socket. A putter shaft may be attached to any point in the head.

c. Grip The grip consists of that part of the shaft designed to be held by the player and any material added to it for the purpose of obtaining a firm hold. The grip shall be substantially straight and plain in form and shall not be moulded for any part of the hands.

d. Clubhead The distance from the heel to the toe of the clubhead shall be greater than the distance from the face to the back. The clubhead shall be generally plain in shape.

The clubhead shall have only one face designed for striking the ball, except that a putter may have two such faces if their characteristics are the same, they are opposite each other and the loft of each is the same and does not exceed ten degrees.

e. Club Face The face shall not have any degree of concavity and, in relation to the ball, shall be hard and rigid. It shall be generally smooth except for such markings as are permitted by Appendix II. If the basic structural material of the head and face of a club,

continued

other than a putter, is metal, no inset or attachment is permitted.

f. Wear A club which conforms with Rule 4-1 when new is deemed to conform after wear through normal use. Any part of a club which has been purposely altered is regarded as new and must conform, in the altered state, with the Rules.

g. Damage If a player's club ceases to conform with Rule 4-1 because of damage sustained in the normal course of play, the player may:
(i) use the club in its damaged state, but only for the remainder of the stipulated round during which such damage was sustained; or
(ii) without unduly delaying play, repair it.
A club which ceases to conform because of damage sustained other than in the normal course of play shall not subsequently be used during the round.
(Damage changing playing characteristics of club — see Rule 4-2.)

4-2.
Playing Characteristics Changed

During a stipulated round, the playing characteristics of a club shall not be purposely changed.
If the playing characteristics of a player's club are changed during a round because of damage sustained in the normal course of play, the player may:
(i) use the club in its altered state; or
(ii) without unduly delaying play, repair it.
If the playing characteristics of a player's club are changed because of damage sustained other than in the normal course of play, the club shall not subsequently be used during the round.
Damage to a club which occurred prior to a round may be repaired during the round, provided the playing characteristics are not changed and play is not unduly delayed.

Rule 4-3.
Foreign Material

No foreign material shall be applied to the club face for the purpose of influencing the movement of the ball.

PENALTY FOR BREACH OF RULE 4-1, -2 or -3: *Disqualification.*

Rule 4-4.
Maximum of Fourteen Clubs

a. Selection and Replacement of Clubs
The player shall start a stipulated round with not more than fourteen clubs. He is limited to the clubs thus selected for that round except that, without unduly delaying play, he may:
(i) if he started with fewer than fourteen, add as many as will bring his total to that number; and
(ii) replace, with any club, a club which becomes unfit for play in the normal course of play.

b. Borrowing or Sharing Clubs
The addition or replacement of a club or clubs may be made by borrowing from anyone; only the borrower may use such club or clubs for the remainder of the round.
The sharing of a club or clubs is prohibited except that partners may share clubs, provided that the total number of clubs carried by the partners so sharing does not exceed fourteen.

PENALTY FOR BREACH OF RULE 4-4a or b,
REGARDLESS OF NUMBER OF EXCESS CLUBS CARRIED:
Match play — *At the conclusion of the hole at which the breach is discovered, the state of the match shall be adjusted by deducting one hole for each hole at which a breach occurred. Maximum deduction per round: two holes.*
Stroke play — *Two strokes for each hole at which any breach occurred; maximum penalty per round: four strokes.*
Bogey and par competitions — *Penalties as in match play.*
Stableford competitions — *see Note to Rule 32-1b.*

Oh dear I've broken my club. What a pity I can't borrow a replacement from my brother who's playing the seventeenth.

It's all right. You can borrow from him provided he doesn't use it again during the course of the round.

c. Excess Club Declared Out of Play

Any club carried or used in breach of this Rule shall be declared out of play by the player immediately upon discovery that a breach has occurred and thereafter shall not be used by the player during the round.

PENALTY FOR BREACH OF RULE 4-4c: *Disqualification.*

RULE 5. The Ball

Rule 5-1.
General

The ball the player uses shall conform to specifications set forth in Appendix III on maximum weight, minimum size, spherical symmetry, initial velocity and overall distance when tested under specified conditions.

Note: In laying down the conditions under which a competition is to be played (Rule 33-1), the Committee may stipulate that the ball to be used shall be of certain specifications, provided these specifications are within the limits prescribed by Appendix III, and that it be of a size, brand and marking as detailed on the current List of Conforming Golf Balls issued by the Royal and Ancient Golf Club of St. Andrews.

No foreign material shall be applied to a ball for the purpose of changing its playing characteristics.

PENALTY FOR BREACH OF RULE 5-1 or 5-2: *Disqualification.*

A ball is unfit for play if it is visibly cut, cracked or out of shape. A ball is not unfit for play solely because mud or other materials adhere to it, its surface is scratched or scraped or its paint is damaged or discoloured.

If a player has reason to believe his ball has become unfit for play during play of the hole being played, he may during the play of such hole lift his ball without penalty to determine whether it is unfit, provided he announces his intention in advance to his opponent in match play or his marker or a fellow-competitor in stroke play and gives his opponent, marker or fellow-competitor an opportunity to examine the ball. If he lifts the ball without announcing his intention in advance or giving his opponent, marker or fellow-competitor an opportunity to examine the ball, *he shall incur a penalty of one stroke.*

If it is determined that the ball has become unfit for play during play of the hole being played, the player may substitute another ball, placing it on the spot where the original ball lay. Otherwise, the original ball shall be replaced.

If a ball breaks into pieces as a result of a stroke, the stroke shall be replayed without penalty (see Rule 20-5).

*PENALTY FOR BREACH OF RULE 5-3:
Match play — Loss of hole; Stroke play — Two strokes.

If a player incurs the general penalty for breach of Rule 5-3, no additional penalty under the Rule shall be applied.

Note 1: The ball may not be cleaned to determine whether it is unfit for play — see Rule 21.

Note 2: If the opponent, marker or fellow-competitor wishes to dispute a claim of unfitness, he must do so before the player plays another ball.

Ball Unfit for Play

Handicap Stroke Play

Definition

A "marker" is one who is appointed by the Committee to record a competitor's score in stroke play. He may be a fellow-competitor. He is not a referee.
A marker should not lift a ball or mark its position unless authorised to do so by the competitor and, unless he is a fellow-competitor, should not attend the flagstick or stand at the hole or mark its position.

Rule 6-1.
Conditions of Competition

The player is responsible for knowing the conditions under which the competition is to be played (Rule 33-1).

Rule 6-2.
Handicap

a. Match Play
Before starting a match in a handicap competition, the players should determine from one another their respective handicaps. If a player begins the match having declared a higher handicap which would affect the number of strokes given or received, *he shall be disqualified;* otherwise, the player shall play off the declared handicap.

b. Stroke Play
In any round of a handicap competition, the competitor shall ensure that his handicap is recorded on his score card before it is returned to the Committee. If no handicap is recorded on his score card before it is returned, or if the recorded handicap is higher than that to which he is entitled and this affects the number of strokes received, *he shall be disqualified* from that round of the handicap competition; otherwise, the score shall stand.

Note: It is the player's responsibility to know the holes at which handicap strokes are to be given or received.

Rule 6-3.
Time of Starting and Groups

a. Time of Starting
The player shall start at the time laid down by the Committee.
b. Groups
In stroke play, the competitor shall remain throughout the round in the group arranged by the Committee unless the Committee authorises or ratifies a change.

continued

PENALTY FOR BREACH OF RULE 6-3: *Disqualification*
(Best-ball and four-ball play — See Rules 30-3a and 31-2.)
Note: The Committee may provide in the conditions of a competition (Rule 33-1) that, if the player arrives at his starting point, ready to play, within five minutes after his starting time, in the absence of circumstances which warrant waiving the penalty of disqualification as provided in Rule 33-7, the penalty for failure to start on time is *loss of the first hole in match play or two strokes at the first hole in stroke play* instead of disqualification.

Rule 6-4.
Caddie

The player may have only one <u>caddie</u> at any one time, *under penalty of disqualification.*
For any breach of a Rule by his caddie, the player incurs the applicable penalty.

Rule 6-5.
Ball

The responsibility for playing the proper ball rests with the player. Each player should put an identification mark on his ball.

Rule 6-6.
Scoring in Stroke Play

a. Recording Scores
After each hole the <u>marker</u> should check the score with the competitor and record it. On completion of the round the marker shall sign the card and hand it to the competitor. If more than one marker records the scores, each shall sign for the part for which he is responsible.

b. Signing and Returning Card
After completion of the round, the competitor should check his score for each hole and settle any doubtful points with the Committee. He shall ensure that the marker has signed the card, countersign the card himself and return it to the Committee as soon as possible.
PENALTY FOR BREACH OF RULE 6-6b: *Disqualification.*

c. Alteration of Card
No alteration may be made on a card after the competitor has returned it to the Committee.

d. Wrong Score for Hole
The competitor is responsible for the correctness of the score recorded for each hole. If he returns a score for any hole lower than actually taken, *he shall be disqualified.* If he returns a score for any hole higher than actually taken, the score as returned shall stand.
Note 1: The Committee is responsible for the addition of scores and application of the handicap recorded on the card — see Rule 33-5.
Note 2: In four-ball stroke play, see also Rule 31-4 and -7a.

Rule 6-7.
Undue Delay

The player shall play without undue delay. Between completion of a hole and playing from the next teeing ground, the player shall not unduly delay play.

PENALTY FOR BREACH OF RULE 6-7:
Match play — Loss of hole; Stroke play — Two Strokes.
For repeated offence — Disqualification.
If the player unduly delays play between holes, he is delaying the play of the next hole and the penalty applies to that hole.

Rule 6-8.
Discontinuance of Play

a. When Permitted

The player shall not discontinue play unless:

(i)   the Committee has suspended play;

(ii)   he believes there is danger from lightning;

(iii)   he is seeking a decision from the Committee on a doubtful or disputed point (see Rules 2-5 and 34-3); or

(iv)   there is some other good reason such as sudden illness.

Bad weather is not of itself a good reason for discontinuing play. If the player discontinues play without specific permission from the Committee, he shall report to the Committee as soon as practicable. If he does so and the Committee considers his reason satisfactory, the player incurs no penalty. Otherwise, *the player shall be disqualified.*

Exception in match play: Players discontinuing match play by agreement are not subject to disqualification unless by so doing the competition is delayed.

Note: Leaving the course does not of itself constitute discontinuance of play.

b. Procedure When Play Suspended by Committee

When play is suspended by the Committee, if the players in a match or group are between the play of two holes, they shall not resume play until the Committee has ordered a resumption of play. If they are in the process of playing a hole, they may continue provided they do so without delay. If they choose to continue, they shall discontinue either before or immediately after completing the hole, and shall not thereafter resume play until the Committee has ordered a resumption of play.

PENALTY FOR BREACH OF RULE 6-8b: *Disqualification.*

c. Lifting Ball When Play Discontinued

When during the play of a hole a player discontinues play under Rule 6-8a, he may lift his ball. A ball may be cleaned when so lifted. If a ball has been so lifted, the player shall, when play is resumed, place a ball on the spot from which the original ball was lifted.

PENALTY FOR BREACH OF RULE 6-8c:

     Match play — Loss of hole; Stroke play — Two strokes.

RULE 7. Practice

Rule 7-1.
Before or Between Rounds

a. Match Play

On any day of a match play competition, a player may practise on the competition <u>course</u> before a round.

b. Stroke Play

On any day of a stroke competition or play-off, a competitor shall not practise on the competition <u>course</u> or test the surface of any putting green on the course before a round or play-off. When two or more rounds of a stroke competition are to be played over consecutive days, practice between those rounds on any competition course remaining to be played is prohibited.

Exception: Practice putting or chipping on or near the first teeing <u>ground</u> before starting a round or play-off is permitted.

PENALTY FOR BREACH OF RULE 7-1b:
Disqualification

Note: The Committee may in the conditions of a competition (Rule 33-1) prohibit practice on the competition course on any day of a match play competition or permit practice on the competition course or part of the course (Rule 33-2c) on any day of or between rounds of a stroke competition.

Rule 7-2.
During Round

A player shall not play a practice <u>stroke</u> either during the play of a hole or between the play of two holes except that, between the play of two holes, the player may practise putting or chipping on or near the <u>putting green</u> of the hole last played, any practice putting green or the <u>teeing ground</u> of the next hole to be played in the round, provided such practice stroke is not played from a hazard and does not unduly delay play (Rule 6-7).

Exception: When play has been suspended by the Committee, a player may, prior to resumption of play, practise (a) as provided in this Rule, (b) anywhere other than on the competition course and (c) as otherwise permitted by the Committee.

PENALTY FOR BREACH OF RULE 7-2:

Match play — Loss of hole; Stroke play — Two strokes.

In the event of a breach between the play of two holes, the penalty applies to the next hole.

Note 1: A practice swing is not a practice <u>stroke</u> and may be taken at any place, provided the player does not breach the Rules.

Note 2: The Committee may prohibit practice on or near the <u>putting green</u> of the hole last played.

Practice putting and chipping on or near the tee of the next hole to be played is permitted as long as play is not delayed.

Definition

"Advice" is any counsel or suggestion which could influence a player in determining his play, the choice of a club or the method of making a stroke.

Information on the Rules or on matters of public information, such as the position of hazards or the flagstick on the putting green, is not advice.

Rule 8-1.
Advice

A player shall not give advice to anyone in the competition except his partner. A player may ask for advice from only his partner or either of their caddies.

My distance chart shows that it is 150 yards from this bunker to the green. I can use this information as distance charts are permissible.

Yes. But if you had asked me what club to use you would have been penalised for seeking advice. (Rule 8-1).

Rule 8-2.
Indicating Line of Play

a. Other Than on Putting Green

Except on the putting green, a player may have the line of play indicated to him by anyone, but no one shall stand on or close to the line while the stroke is being played. Any mark placed during the play of a hole by the player or with his knowledge to indicate the line shall be removed before the stroke is played.

Exception: Flagstick attended or held up — See Rule 17-1.

b. On the Putting Green

When the player's ball is on the putting green, the player, his partner or either of their caddies may, before but not during the stroke, point out a line for putting, but in so doing the putting green shall not be touched. No mark shall be placed anywhere to indicate a line for putting.

PENALTY FOR BREACH OF RULE:
Match play — Loss of hole; Stroke play — Two strokes.
Note: In a team competition without concurrent individual competition, the Committee may in the conditions of the competition (Rule 33-1) permit each team to appoint one person, e.g., team captain or coach, who may give advice (including pointing out a line for putting) to members of that team. Such person shall be identified to the Committee prior to the start of the competition.

On the putting green, only the pla[...] caddie, his partner or his partners c[...] may point out a line for putting[...]

Rule 9-1.
General

The number of strokes a player has taken shall include any penalty strokes incurred.

Rule 9-2.
Match Play

A player who has incurred a penalty shall inform his opponent as soon as practicable. If he fails to do so, he shall be deemed to have given wrong information, even if he was not aware that he had incurred a penalty.

An opponent is entitled to ascertain from the player, during the play of a hole, the number of strokes he has taken and, after play of a hole, the number of strokes taken on the hole just completed. If during the play of a hole the player gives or is deemed to give wrong information as to the number of strokes taken, he shall incur no penalty if he corrects the mistake before his opponent has played his next stroke. If the player fails so to correct the wrong information, *he shall lose the hole.*

If after play of a hole the player gives or is deemed to give wrong information as to the number of strokes taken on the hole just completed and this affects the opponent's understanding of the result of the hole, he shall incur no penalty if he corrects his mistake before any player plays from the next teeing ground or, in the case of the last hole of the match, before all players leave the putting green. If the player fails so to correct the wrong information, *he shall lose the hole.*

Rule 9-3.
Stroke Play

A competitor who has incurred a penalty should inform his marker as soon as practicable.

ORDER OF PLAY

RULE 10 Order of Play

Rule 10-1.
Match Play

a. Teeing Ground
The side entitled to play first from the teeing ground is said to have the "honour". The side which shall have the honour at the first teeing ground shall be determined by the order of the draw. In the absence of a draw, the honour should be decided by lot.
The side which wins a hole shall take the honour at the next teeing ground. If a hole has been halved, the side which had the honour at the previous teeing ground shall retain it.

b. Other Than on Teeing Ground
When the balls are in play, the ball farther from the hole shall be played first. If the balls are equidistant from the hole, the ball to be played first should be decided by lot.
Exception: Rule 30-3c (best-ball and four-ball match play).

c. Playing Out of Turn
If a player plays when his opponent should have played, the opponent may immediately require the player to cancel the stroke and play a ball in correct order, without penalty (see Rule 20-5).

Rule 10-2. *Stroke Play*	**a. Teeing Ground** The competitor entitled to play first from the teeing ground is said to have the "honour". The competitor who shall have the honour at the first teeing ground shall be determined by the order of the draw. In the absence of a draw, the honour should be decided by lot. The competitor with the lowest score at a hole shall take the honour at the next teeing ground. The competitor with the second lowest score shall play next and so on. If two or more competitors have the same score at a hole, they shall play from the next teeing ground in the same order as at the previous teeing ground. **b. Other Than on Teeing Ground** When the balls are in play, the ball farthest from the hole shall be played first. If two or more balls are equidistant from the hole, the ball to be played first should be decided by lot. *Exceptions:* Rules 22 (ball interfering with or assisting play) and 31-5 (four-ball stroke play). **c. Playing Out of Turn** If a competitor plays out of turn, no penalty is incurred and the ball shall be played as it lies. If, however, the Committee determines that competitors have agreed to play in an order other than that set forth in Clauses 2a and 2b of this Rule to give one of them an advantage, *they shall be disqualified.* (Incorrect order of play in threesomes and foursomes stroke play — see Rule 29-3.)
Rule 10-3. *Provisional Ball or Second Ball* *from Teeing Ground*	If a player plays a provisional ball or a second ball from a teeing ground, he should do so after his opponent or fellow-competitor has played his first stroke. If a player plays a provisional ball or a second ball out of turn, Clauses 1c and 2c of this Rule shall apply.
Rule 10-4. *Ball Moved in Measuring*	If a ball is moved in measuring to determine which ball is farther from the hole, no penalty is incurred and the ball shall be replaced.

TEEING GROUND

RULE 11 Teeing Ground

Definition	The "teeing ground" is the starting place for the hole to be played. It is a rectangular area two club-lengths in depth, the front and the sides of which are defined by the outside limits of two tee-markers. A ball is outside the teeing ground when all of it lies outside the teeing ground.
Rule 11-1. *Teeing*	In teeing, the ball may be placed on the ground, on an irregularity of surface created by the player on the ground or on a tee, sand or other substance in order to raise it off the ground. A player may stand outside the teeing ground to play a ball within it.

Before a player plays his first stroke with any ball from the teeing ground of the hole being played, the tee-markers are deemed to be fixed. In such circumstances, if the player moves or allows to be moved a tee-marker for the purpose of avoiding interference with his stance, the area of his intended swing or his line of play, *he shall incur the penalty for a breach of Rule 13-2.*

Rule 11-2.
Tee-Markers

Teeing Ground

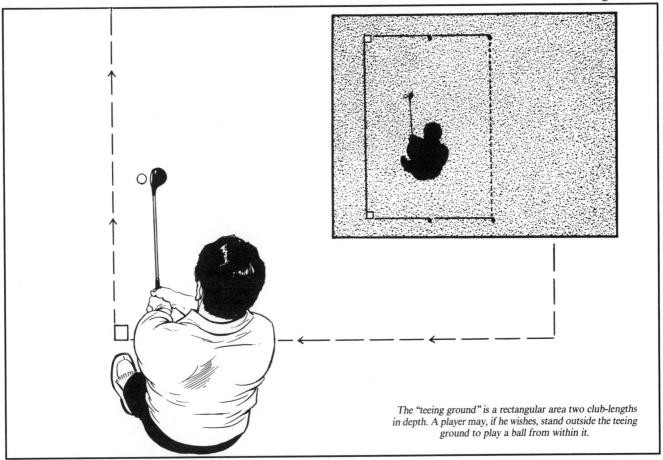

The "teeing ground" is a rectangular area two club-lengths in depth. A player may, if he wishes, stand outside the teeing ground to play a ball from within it.

If a ball, when not in play, falls off a tee or is knocked off a tee by the player in addressing it, it may be re-teed without penalty, but if a stroke is made at the ball in these circumstances, whether the ball is moving or not, the stroke counts but no penalty is incurred.

11-3.
Ball Falling Off Tee

a. Match Play
If a player, when starting a hole, plays a ball from outside the teeing ground, the opponent may immediately require the player to cancel the stroke so played and play a ball from within the teeing ground, without penalty.

b. Stroke Play
If a competitor, when starting a hole, plays a ball from outside the teeing ground, *he shall incur a penalty of two strokes* and shall then play a ball from within the teeing ground.

If the competitor plays a stroke from the next teeing ground without first correcting his mistake or, in the case of the last hole of the round, leaves the putting green without first declaring his intention to correct his mistake, *he shall be disqualified.*

Strokes played by a competitor from outside the teeing ground do not count in his score.

11-4.
Playing Outside Teeing Ground

31

RULE 12 PLAYING THE BALL

Searching for and Identifying Ball

Rule 12-1.
Searching for Ball; Seeing Ball

In searching for his ball anywhere on the course, the player may touch or bend long grass, rushes, bushes, whins, heather or the like, but only to the extent necessary to find and identify it, provided that this does not improve the lie of the ball, the area of his intended swing or his line of play.

A player is not necessarily entitled to see his ball when playing a stroke.

In a hazard, if a ball is covered by loose impediments or sand, the player may remove by probing, raking or other means as much thereof as will enable him to see a part of the ball. If an excess is removed, no penalty is incurred and the ball shall be re-covered so that only a part of the ball is visible. If the ball is moved in such removal, no penalty is incurred; the ball shall be replaced and, if necessary, re-covered. As to removal of loose impediments outside a hazard, see Rule 23.

If a ball lying in casual water, ground under repair or a hole, cast or runway made by a burrowing animal, a reptile or a bird is accidentally moved during search, no penalty is incurred; the ball shall be replaced, unless the player elects to proceed under Rule 25-1b.

If a ball is believed to be lying in water in a water hazard, the player may probe for it with a club or otherwise. If the ball is moved in so doing, no penalty is incurred; the ball shall be replaced, unless the player elects to proceed under Rule 26-1.

Definitions

A "hazard" is any bunker or water hazard.

A "bunker" is a hazard consisting of a prepared area of ground, often a hollow, from which turf or soil has been removed and replaced with sand or the like. Grass-covered ground bordering or within a bunker is not part of the bunker. The margin of a bunker extends vertically downwards, but not upwards.

A "water hazard" is any sea, lake, pond, river, ditch, surface drainage ditch or other open water course (whether or not containing water) and anything of a similar nature.

All ground or water within the margin of a water hazard is part of the water hazard. The margin of a water hazard extends vertically upwards and downwards. Stakes and lines defining the margins of water hazards are in the hazards.

PENALTY FOR BREACH OF RULE 12-1:
Match play — Loss of hole; Stroke play — Two strokes

Removal of leaves in hazard
Seeing part of the ball

Searching for ball in Bunkers

Rule 12-2.
Identifying Ball

The responsibility for playing the proper ball rests with the player. Each player should put an identification mark on his ball. Except in a hazard, the player may, without penalty, lift a ball he believes to be his own for the purpose of identification and clean it to the extent necessary for identification. If the ball is the player's ball, he shall replace it. Before the player lifts the ball, he shall announce his intention to his opponent in match play or his marker or a fellow-competitor in stroke play and give his opponent, marker or fellow-competitor an opportunity to observe the lifting and replacement. If he lifts his ball without announcing his intention in advance or giving his opponent, marker or fellow-competitor an opportunity to observe, or if he lifts his ball for identification in a hazard, *he shall incur a penalty of one stroke* and the ball shall be replaced.

If a player who is required to replace a ball fails to do so, *he shall incur the penalty for a breach of Rule 20-3a, but no additional penalty under Rule 12-2 shall be applied.*

RULE 13.

Ball Played As It Lies;

Lie, Area of Intended Swing and Line of Play; Stance

Definitions

A "hazard" is any bunker or water hazard.

A "bunker" is a hazard consisting of a prepared area of ground, often a hollow, from which turf or soil has been removed and replaced with sand or the like. Grass-covered ground bordering or within a bunker is not part of the bunker. The margin of a bunker extends vertically downwards, but not upwards.

A "water hazard" is any sea, lake, pond, river, ditch, surface drainage ditch or other open water course (whether or not containing water) and anything of a similar nature.

All ground or water within the margin of a water hazard is part of the water hazard. The margin of a water hazard extends vertically upwards and downwards. Stakes and lines defining the margins of water hazards are in the hazards.

Rule 13-1.
Ball Played As It Lies

The ball shall be played as it lies, except as otherwise provided in the Rules. (Ball at rest moved — see Rule 18.)

Rule 13-2.
Improving Lie, Area of Intended Swing or Line of Play

Except as provided in the Rules, a player shall not improve or allow to be improved:
    the position or lie of his ball,
    the area of his intended swing,
    his line of play or
    the area in which he is to drop or place a ball
by any of the following actions:
    moving, bending or breaking anything growing or fixed (including immovable obstructions and objects defining out of bounds) or
    removing or pressing down sand, loose soil, replaced divots, other cut turf placed in position or other irregularities of surface
except as follows:
    as may occur in fairly taking his stance,
    in making a stroke or the backward movement of his club for a stroke,
    on the teeing ground in creating or eliminating irregularities of surface, or
    on the putting green in removing sand and loose soil as provided in Rule 16-1a or in repairing damage as provided in Rule 16-1c.
The club may be grounded only lightly and shall not be pressed on the ground.
Exception: Ball lying in or touching hazard — see Rule 13-4.

A player must not move, bend
or break anything growing or fixed.

Sand on the putting green is a loose
impediment and may be removed. (Rule
16-1a (i) and Definition of
"Loose Impediment.")

Improving Line of Play

*It is not permitted to remove loose sand on the fringe
or apron of the green.*
(See Definition of "Loose Impediment").

Rule 13-3.
Building Stance

A player is entitled to place his feet firmly in taking his stance, but he shall not build a stance.

Rule 13-4.
Ball Lying in or Touching Hazard

Except as provided in the Rules, before making a stroke at a ball which lies in or touches a hazard (whether a bunker or a water hazard), the player shall not:
a. Test the condition of the hazard or any similar hazard,
b. Touch the ground in the hazard or water in the water hazard with a club or otherwise, or
c. Touch or move a loose impediment lying in or touching the hazard.
Exceptions:
1. At address or in the backward movement for the stroke, the club may touch any obstruction or any grass, bush, tree or other growing thing.
2. The player may place his clubs in a hazard, provided nothing is done which may constitute testing the soil or improving the lie of the ball.
3. The player after playing the stroke, or his caddie at any time without the authority of the player, may smooth sand or soil in the hazard, provided that, if the ball still lies in the hazard, nothing is done which improves the lie of the ball or assists the player in his subsequent play of the hole.

PENALTY FOR BREACH OF RULE:
Match play — Loss of hole; Stroke play — Two strokes.
(Searching for ball — see Rule 12-1.)

Ball Lying in Bunker
Before making a stroke at a ball which lies in a bunker the player shall not

touch the ground with his club

smooth the sand or soil

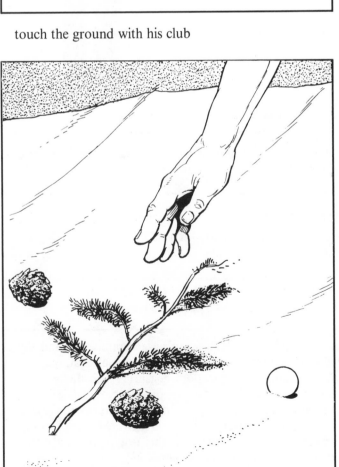

remove loose impediments

touch a loose impediment with his club at address or on his backswing

RULE 14.

Striking the Ball

Definition

A "stroke" is the forward movement of the club made with the intention of fairly striking at and moving the ball, but if a player checks his downswing voluntarily before the clubhead reaches the ball he is deemed not to have made a stroke.

Rule 14-1.
Ball to be Fairly Struck At

The ball shall be fairly struck at with the head of the club and must not be pushed, scraped or spooned.

Rule 14-2.
Assistance

In making a stroke, a player shall not accept physical assistance or protection from the elements.

PENALTY FOR BREACH OF RULE 14-1 or -2:
Match play — Loss of hole; Stroke play — Two strokes.

Rule 14-3.
Artificial Devices and
Unusual Equipment

Except as provided in the Rules, during a stipulated round the player shall not use any artificial device or unusual equipment:
a. For the purpose of gauging or measuring the distance or conditions which might affect his play; or
b. Which might assist him in gripping the club, in making a stroke or in his play, except that plain gloves may be worn, resin, tape or gauze may be applied to the grip (provided such application does not render the grip non-conforming under Rule 4-1c) and a towel or handkerchief may be wrapped around the grip.

PENALTY FOR BREACH OF RULE 14-3: *Disqualification.*

If a player's club strikes the ball more than once in the course of a stroke, the player shall count the stroke and *add a penalty stroke*, making two strokes in all.

Rule 14-4.
Striking the Ball More than Once

A player shall not play while his ball is moving.
Exceptions:
    Ball falling off tee — Rule 11-3.
    Striking the ball more than once — Rule 14-4.
    Ball moving in water — Rule 14-6.
When the ball begins to move only after the player has begun the stroke or the backward movement of his club for the stroke, he shall incur no penalty under this Rule for playing a moving ball, but he is not exempt from any penalty incurred under the following Rules:
    Ball at rest moved by player — Rule 18-2a.
    Ball at rest moving after address — Rule 18-2b.
    Ball at rest moving after loose impediment touched — Rule 18-2c.

Rule 14-5.
Playing Moving Ball

When a ball is moving in water in a water hazard, the player may, without penalty, make a stroke, but he must not delay making his stroke in order to allow the wind or current to improve the position of the ball. A ball moving in water in a water hazard may be lifted if the player elects to invoke Rule 26.

Rule 14-6.
Ball Moving in Water

PENALTY FOR BREACH OF RULE 14-5 or -6:
Match play — Loss of hole; Stroke play — Two strokes.

RULE 15.

Playing a Wrong Ball

Definition

A "wrong ball" is any ball other than:
a. The ball in play,
b. A provisional ball or
c. In stroke play, a second ball played under Rule 3-3 or Rule 20-7b.
Note: Ball in play includes a ball substituted for the ball in play when the player is proceeding under an applicable Rule which does not permit substitution.

A player must hole out with the ball played from the teeing ground unless a Rule permits him to substitute another ball. If a player substitutes another ball when proceeding under an applicable Rule which does not permit substitution, that ball is not a wrong ball; it becomes the ball in play and, if the error is not corrected as provided in Rule 20-6, *the player shall incur a penalty of loss of hole in match play or two strokes in stroke play.*

Rule 15-1.
General

If a player plays a stroke with a wrong ball except in a hazard, *he shall lose the hole.*

continued

Rule 15-2.
Match Play

If a player plays any strokes in a hazard with a wrong ball, there is no penalty. Strokes played in a hazard with a wrong ball do not count in the player's score. If the wrong ball belongs to another player, its owner shall place a ball on the spot from which the wrong ball was first played.

If the player and opponent exchange balls during the play of a hole, the first to play the wrong ball other than from a hazard shall lose the hole; when this cannot be determined, the hole shall be played out with the balls exchanged.

Rule 15-3.
Stroke Play

If a competitor plays a stroke or strokes with a wrong ball, *he shall incur a penalty of two strokes,* unless the only stroke or strokes played with such ball were played when it was lying in a hazard, in which case no penalty is incurred.

The competitor must correct his mistake by playing the correct ball. If he fails to correct his mistake before he plays a stroke from the next teeing ground or, in the case of the last hole of the round, fails to declare his intention to correct his mistake before leaving the putting green, *he shall be disqualified.*

Strokes played by a competitor with a wrong ball do not count in his score.

If the wrong ball belongs to another competitor, its owner shall place a ball on the spot from which the wrong ball was first played.

(Lie of ball to be placed or replaced altered — see Rule 20-3b.)

Playing a Substituted Ball

I cleaned my ball but I've just noticed I didn't put the right ball down. I had another one in my pocket and that's the one I have played.

Although the Rule does not allow you to substitute a ball it is still the ball in play, but you incur a 2 stroke penalty.

Definitions

The "putting green" is all ground of the hole being played which is specially prepared for putting or otherwise defined as such by the Committee. A ball is on the putting green when any part of it touches the putting green.

A ball is "holed" when it is at rest within the circumference of the hole and all of it is below the level of the lip of the hole.

Rule 16-1.
General

a. Touching Line of Putt

The line of putt must not be touched except:

(i)   the player may move sand and loose soil on the putting green and other loose impediments by picking them up or by brushing them aside with his hand or a club without pressing anything down;

(ii) in addressing the ball, the player may place the club in front of the ball without pressing anything down;

(iii) in measuring — Rule 10-4;

(iv) in lifting the ball — Rule 16-1b;

(v)   in pressing down a ball-marker;

(vi) in repairing old hole plugs or ball marks on the putting green — Rule 16-1c; and

(vii) in removing movable obstructions — Rule 24-1.

(Indicating line for putting on putting green — See Rule 8-2b.)

Continued

Touching Line of Putt

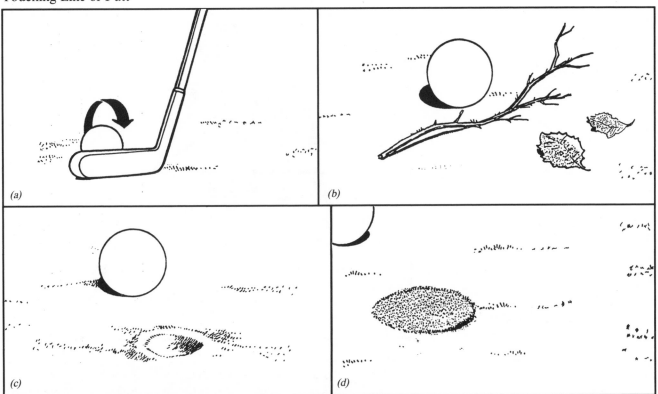

Examples of when the line of putt may be touched without penalty:

(a) placing clubhead in front of the ball without pressing anything down when addressing the ball
(b) removing a loose impediment, such as a twig or leaf
(c) repairing a ball mark
(d) repairing an old hole plug

b. Lifting Ball

A ball on the putting green may be lifted and, if desired, cleaned. A ball so lifted shall be replaced on the spot from which it was lifted.

c. Repair of Hole Plugs and Ball Marks

The player may repair an old hole plug or damage to the putting green caused by the impact of a ball, whether or not the player's ball lies on the putting green. If the ball is moved in the process of such repair, it shall be replaced, without penalty.

d. Testing Surface

During the play of a hole, a player shall not test the surface of the putting green by rolling a ball or roughening or scraping the surface.

e. Standing Astride or on Line of Putt

The player shall not make a stroke on the putting green from a stance astride, or with either foot touching, the line of the putt or an extension of that line behind the ball. For the purpose of this Clause only, the line of putt does not extend beyond the hole.

f. Position of Caddie or Partner

While making the stroke, the player shall not allow his caddie, his partner or his partner's caddie to position himself on or close to an extension of the line of putt behind the ball.

g. Playing Stroke While Another Ball in Motion

A player shall not play a stroke while another ball is in motion after a stroke on the putting green.

(Lifting ball interfering with or assisting play while another ball in motion — see Rule 22.)

PENALTY FOR BREACH OF RULE 16-1:
Match play — Loss of hole;
Stroke play — Two strokes.

Cleaning Ball Testing Surface

There is nothing in the Rules which prohibits a player from cleaning a ball by rubbing it on the surface of the green provided that the conditions of Rule 16-1d are observed.

Rule 16-2.
Ball Overhanging Hole

When any part of the ball overhangs the lip of the hole, the player is allowed enough time to reach the hole without unreasonable delay and an additional ten seconds to determine whether the ball is at rest. If by then the ball has not fallen into the hole, it is deemed to be at rest. If the ball subsequently falls into the hole, the player is deemed to have holed out with his last stroke, and *he*
continued

Ball Overhanging Hole

Lifting and Marking Ball: Procedure

Rule 16-2. continued

shall add a penalty stroke to his score for the hole; otherwise there is no penalty under this Rule.
(Undue delay — see Rule 6-7.)

RULE 17.

The Flagstick

Rule 17-1.
Flagstick Attended, Removed or Held Up

Before and during the <u>stroke</u>, the player may have the flagstick attended, removed or held up to indicate the position of the hole. This may be done only on the authority of the player before he plays his stroke.

If the flagstick is attended, removed or held up by an opponent, a fellow-competitor or the caddie of either with the player's knowledge and no objection is made, the player shall be deemed to have authorised it. If a player or a caddie attends, removes or holds up the flagstick or stands near the hole while a stroke is being played, he shall be deemed to be attending the flagstick until the ball comes to rest.

If the flagstick is not attended before the stroke is played, it shall not be attended or removed while the ball is in motion.

Adjustment of the Flagstick — player's ball off the green

It is permissible to hold the flagstick with one hand and to putt with the other provided the flagstick has been removed and the ball therefore does not strike it.

Flagstick held up to indicate Position of Hole

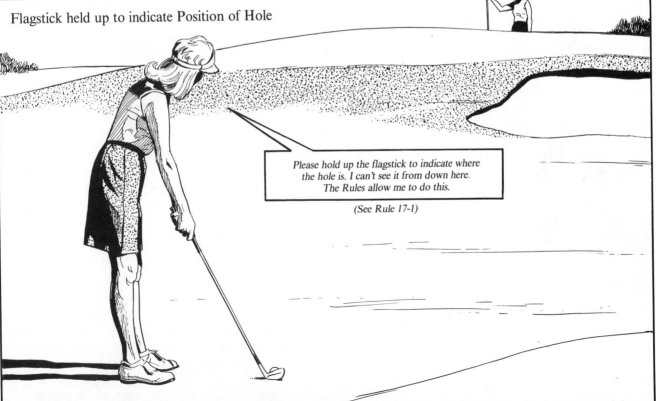

Please hold up the flagstick to indicate where the hole is. I can't see it from down here. The Rules allow me to do this.

(See Rule 17-1)

Rule 17-2.
Unauthorised Attendance

a. Match Play

In match play, an opponent or his caddie shall not attend, remove or hold up the flagstick without the player's knowledge or authority while the player is making a stroke or his ball is in motion.

b. Stroke Play

In stroke play, if a fellow-competitor or his caddie attends, removes or holds up the flagstick without the competitor's knowledge or authority while the competitor is making a stroke or his ball is in motion, *the fellow-competitor shall incur the penalty* for breach of this Rule. In such circumstances, if the competitor's ball strikes the flagstick or the person attending it, the competitor incurs no penalty and the ball shall be played as it lies, except that, if the stroke was played from the putting green, the stroke shall be replayed.

PENALTY FOR BREACH OF RULE 17-1 or -2:
Match play — Loss of hole; Stroke play — Two strokes.

Rule 17-3.
Ball Striking Flagstick or Attendant

The player's ball shall not strike:
a. The flagstick when attended, removed or held up by the player, his partner or either of their caddies, or by another person with the player's knowledge or authority; or
b. The player's caddie, his partner or his partner's caddie when attending the flagstick, or another person attending the flagstick with the player's knowledge or authority, or equipment carried by any such person; or
c. The flagstick in the hole, unattended, when the ball has been played from the putting green.

PENALTY FOR BREACH OF RULE 17-3:
Match play — Loss of hole; Stroke play — Two strokes,
and the ball shall be played as it lies.

Ball Strikes Flagstick Lying on Green

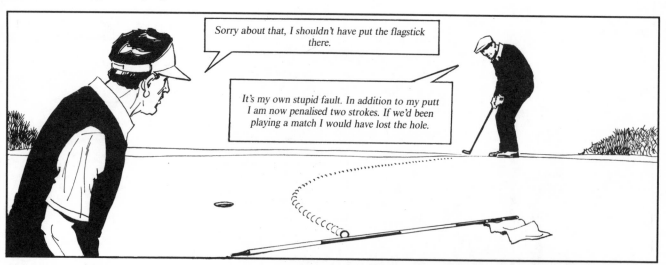

Sorry about that, I shouldn't have put the flagstick there.

It's my own stupid fault. In addition to my putt I am now penalised two strokes. If we'd been playing a match I would have lost the hole.

Rule 17-4.
Ball Resting Against Flagstick

If the ball rests against the flagstick when it is in the hole, the player or another person authorised by him may move or remove the flagstick and if the ball falls into the hole, the player shall be deemed to have holed out at his last stroke; otherwise the ball, if moved, shall be placed on the lip of the hole, without penalty.

Ball at Rest Moved

Definitions

A ball is deemed to have "moved" if it leaves its position and comes to rest in any other place.

An "outside agency" is any agency not part of the match or, in stroke play, not part of a competitor's side, and includes a referee, a marker, an observer or a forecaddie. Neither wind nor water is an outside agency.

"Equipment" is anything used, worn or carried by or for the player except any ball he has played at the hole being played and any small object, such as a coin or a tee, when used to mark the position of a ball or the extent of an area in which a ball is to be dropped. Equipment includes a golf cart, whether or not motorised. If such a cart is shared by more than one player, its status under the Rules is the same as that of a caddie employed by more than one player. See "Caddie".

A player has "addressed the ball" when he has taken his stance and has also grounded his club, except that in a hazard a player has addressed the ball when he has taken his stance.

Taking the "stance" consists in a player placing his feet in position for and preparatory to making a stroke.

Rule 18-1.
By Outside Agency

If a ball at rest is moved by an outside agency, the player shall incur no penalty and the ball shall be replaced before the player plays another stroke.

(Player's ball at rest moved by another ball — see Rule 18-5.)

Rule 18-2.
By Player, Partner, Caddie
or Equipment

a. General

When a player's ball is in play, if:

(i) the player, his partner or either of their caddies lifts or moves it, touches it purposely (except with a club in the act of addressing it) or causes it to move except as permitted by a Rule, or

(ii) equipment of the player or his partner causes the ball to move,

the player shall incur a penalty stroke. The ball shall be replaced unless the movement of the ball occurs after the player has begun his swing and he does not discontinue his swing.

Under the Rules no penalty is incurred if a player accidentally causes his ball to move in the following circumstances:

In measuring to determine which ball farther from hole —Rule 10-4

In searching for covered ball in hazard or for ball in casual water, ground under repair, etc. — Rule 12-1

In the process of repairing hole plug or ball mark — Rule 16-1c

Continued

In the process of removing loose impediment on putting green —Rule 18-2c

In the process of lifting ball under a Rule — Rule 20-1

In the process of placing or replacing ball under a Rule —Rule 20-3a

In complying with Rule 22 relating to lifting ball interfering with or assisting play

In removal of movable obstruction — Rule 24-1.

b. Ball Moving After Address

If a player's ball in play moves after he has addressed it (other than as a result of a stroke), the player shall be deemed to have moved the ball and *shall incur a penalty stroke*. The player shall replace the ball unless the movement of the ball occurs after he has begun his swing and he does not discontinue his swing.

Ball moving after address

My ball moved after I addressed it and it has rolled down hill into a bush. Do I play it from where it now lies?

No. You must replace your ball and add one penalty stroke to your score.

Ball at Rest Moved

Ball at rest moved by outside agency. No penalty. Replace ball before playing next stroke. Wind and water are not outside agencies. If a ball is not immediately recoverable another ball may be substituted (Rule 18-1).

Ball at rest moved by player, partner, caddie or equipment. One stroke penalty. Replace ball. (Rule 18-2a).

Ball moved after loose impediment touched. One stroke penalty. Replace ball. (Rule 18-2c).

Ball moving after address. One stroke penalty. Replace ball. (Rule 18-2b).

Ball at rest moved by opponent or fellow-competitor during search. No penalty. Replace ball. (Rule 18-3a,-4).

c. Ball Moving After Loose Impediment Touched

Through the green, if the ball moves after any loose impediment lying within a club-length of it has been touched by the player, his partner or either of their caddies and before the player has addressed it, the player shall be deemed to have moved the ball and *shall incur a penalty stroke.* The player shall replace the ball unless the movement of the ball occurs after he has begun his swing and he does not discontinue his swing.

On the putting green, if the ball moves in the process of removing any loose impediment, it shall be replaced without penalty.

Rule 18-3.
By Opponent, Caddie or Equipment in Match Play

a. During Search

If, during search for a player's ball, it is moved by an opponent, his caddie or his equipment, no penalty is incurred and the player shall replace the ball.

b. Other Than During Search

If, other than during search for a ball, the ball is touched or moved by an opponent, his caddie or his equipment, except as otherwise provided in the Rules, *the opponent shall incur a penalty stroke.* The player shall replace the ball.

(Ball moved in measuring to determine which ball farther from the hole — see Rule 10-4.)

(Playing a wrong ball — see Rule 15-2.)

(Ball moved in complying with Rule 22 relating to lifting ball interfering with or assisting play.)

Rule 18-4.
By Fellow-Competitor, Caddie or Equipment in Stroke Play

If a competitor's ball is moved by a fellow-competitor, his caddie or his equipment, no penalty is incurred. The competitor shall replace his ball.

(Playing a wrong ball — see Rule 15-3.)

Rule 18-5.
By Another Ball

If a ball in play and at rest is moved by another ball in motion after a stroke, the moved ball shall be replaced.

---

*PENALTY FOR BREACH OF RULE:

Match play — Loss of hole; Stroke play — Two strokes.

*If a player who is required to replace a ball fails to do so, he shall incur the general penalty for breach of Rule 18 but no additional penalty under Rule 18 shall be applied.

Note 1: If a ball to be replaced under this Rule is not immediately recoverable, another ball may be substituted.

Note 2: If it is impossible to determine the spot on which a ball is to be placed, see Rule 20-3c.

RULE 19.

Ball in Motion Deflected or Stopped

Definitions

An "outside agency" is any agency not part of the match or, in stroke play, not part of a competitor's side, and includes a referee, a marker, an observer or a forecaddie. Neither wind nor water is an outside agency.

"Equipment" is anything used, worn or carried by or for the player except any ball he has played at the hole being played and any small object, such as a coin or a tee, when used to mark the position of a ball or the extent of an area in which a ball is to be dropped. Equipment includes a golf cart, whether or not motorised. If such a cart is shared by more than one player, its status under the Rules is the same as that of a caddie employed by more than one player. See "Caddie".

Rule 19-1.
By Outside Agency

If a ball in motion is accidentally deflected or stopped by any outside agency, it is a rub of the green, no penalty is incurred and the ball shall be played as it lies except:

a. If a ball in motion after a stroke other than on the putting green comes to rest in or on any moving or animate outside agency, the player shall, through the green or in a hazard, drop the ball, or on the putting green place the ball, as near as possible to the spot where the outside agency was when the ball came to rest in or on it, and

b. If a ball in motion after a stroke on the putting green is deflected or stopped by, or comes to rest in or on, any moving or animate outside agency except a worm or an insect, the stroke shall be cancelled and the ball shall be replaced.

If the ball is not immediately recoverable, another ball may be substituted.

(Player's ball deflected or stopped by another ball — see Rule 19-5.)

Note: If the referee or the Committee determines that a competitor's ball has been purposely deflected or stopped by an outside agency, Rule 1-4 applies to the competitor. If the outside agency is a fellow-competitor or his caddie, Rule 1-2 applies to the fellow-competitor.

Rule 19-2.
By Player, Partner, Caddie or Equipment

a. Match Play. If a player's ball is accidentally deflected or stopped by himself, his partner or either of their caddies or equipment, *he shall lose the hole.*

b. Stroke Play. If a competitor's ball is accidentally deflected or stopped by himself, his partner or either of their caddies or equipment, *the competitor shall incur a penalty of two strokes.* The ball shall be played as it lies, except when it comes to rest in or on the competitor's, his partner's or either of their caddies' clothes or equipment, in which case the competitor shall through the green or in a hazard drop the ball, or on the putting green place the ball, as near as possible to where the article was when the ball came to rest in or on it.

Exception: Dropped Ball — see Rule 20-2a.

(Ball purposely deflected or stopped by player, partner or caddie — see Rule 1-2.)

If a player's ball is accidentally deflected or stopped by an opponent, his caddie or his <u>equipment</u>, no penalty is incurred. The player may play the ball as it lies or, before another <u>stroke</u> is played by either side, cancel the stroke and replay it (see Rule 20-5). If the player elects to replay the stroke and the original ball is not immediately recoverable, another ball may be substituted.

If the ball has come to rest in or on the opponent's or his caddie's clothes or equipment, the player may <u>through the green</u> or in a <u>hazard</u> drop the ball, or on the putting green place the ball, as near as possible to where the article was when the ball came to rest in or on it.

Exception: Ball striking person attending flagstick — see Rule 17-3b.

(Ball purposely deflected or stopped by opponent or caddie —see Rule 1-2.)

Rule 19-3.
By Opponent, Caddie or Equipment in Match Play

See Rule 19-1 regarding ball deflected by outside agency.

Rule 19-4.
By Fellow-Competitor, Caddie or Equipment in Stroke Play

Ball in Motion Deflected by Fellow-Competitor's Equipment

My ball was deflected by your bag, so I'm going to replay the stroke.

No, you cannot. This is stroke play so you must play your ball as it lies (Rule 19-1). It is only in match play that you have the option to replay the stroke. (Rule 19-3b).

Rule 19-5.
By Another Ball

If a player's ball in motion after a stroke is deflected or stopped by a ball at rest, the player shall play his ball as it lies. In stroke play, if both balls lay on the <u>putting green</u> prior to the stroke, *the player incurs a penalty of two strokes.* Otherwise, no penalty is incurred.

If a player's ball in motion after a stroke is deflected or stopped by another ball in motion, the player shall play his ball as it lies. There is no penalty unless the player was in breach of Rule 16-1g, in which case *he shall incur the penalty for breach of that Rule.*

Exception: Ball in motion after a stroke on the putting green deflected or stopped by moving or animate outside agency — see Rule 19-1b.

PENALTY FOR BREACH OF RULE: Match play — Loss of hole; Stroke play — Two strokes.

RELIEF SITUATIONS AND PROCEDURE
RULE 20

Lifting, Dropping and Placing; Playing from Wrong Place

Rule 20-1.
Lifting

A ball to be lifted under the Rules may be lifted by the player, his partner or another person authorised by the player. In any such case, the player shall be responsible for any breach of the Rules. The position of the ball shall be marked before it is lifted under a Rule which requires it to be replaced. If it is not marked, *the player shall incur a penalty of one stroke* and the ball shall be replaced. If it is not replaced, *the player shall incur the general penalty* for breach of this Rule but no additional penalty under Rule 20-1 shall be applied.

If a ball or a ball-marker is accidentally moved in the process of lifting the ball under a Rule or marking its position, no penalty is incurred and the ball or the ball-marker shall be replaced.

Note: The position of a ball to be lifted should be marked by placing a ball-marker, a small coin or other similar object immediately behind the ball. If the ball-marker interferes with the play, <u>stance</u> or <u>stroke</u> of another player, it should be placed one or more clubhead-lengths to one side.

Rule 20-2.
Dropping and Re-dropping

a. By Whom and How
A ball to be dropped under the Rules shall be dropped by the player himself. He shall stand erect, hold the ball at shoulder height and arm's length and drop it. If a ball is dropped by any other person or in any other manner and the error is not corrected as provided in Rule 20-6, *the player shall incur a penalty stroke.*

If the ball touches the player, his partner, either of their caddies or their equipment before or after it strikes the ground, the ball shall be re-dropped, without penalty. There is no limit to the number of times a ball shall be re-dropped in such circumstances.

(Taking action to influence position or movement of ball — see Rule 1-2.)

b. Where to Drop
When a ball is to be dropped, it shall be dropped as near as possible to the spot where the ball lay, but not nearer the hole, except when a Rule permits or requires it to be dropped elsewhere. If a ball is to be dropped in a <u>hazard</u>, the ball shall be dropped in and come to rest in that hazard.

Note: A ball when dropped must first strike the ground where the applicable Rule requires it to be dropped. If it is not so dropped, Rules 20-6 and -7 apply.

c. When to Re-Drop
A dropped ball shall be re-dropped without penalty if it:
- (i) rolls into a <u>hazard</u>;
- (ii) rolls out of a hazard;
- (iii) rolls onto a <u>putting green</u>;
- (iv) rolls <u>out of bounds</u>;
- (v) rolls back into the condition from which relief was taken under Rule 24-2 (immovable obstruction) or Rule 25 (abnormal ground conditions and wrong putting green);
- (vi) rolls and comes to rest more than two club-lengths from where it first struck the ground; or
- (vii) rolls and comes to rest nearer the hole than its original position unless otherwise permitted by the Rules.

Continued.

> If the ball rolls into such position, it shall be placed as near as possible to spot where it first struck the ground when re-dropped.
> If a ball to be re-dropped or placed under this Rule is not immediately recoverable, another ball may be substituted.

Dropping Ball: How to Drop

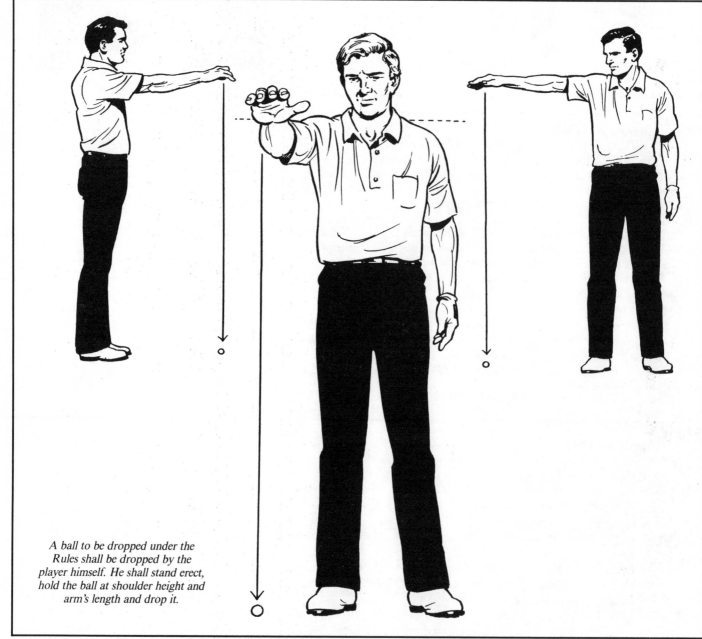

A ball to be dropped under the Rules shall be dropped by the player himself. He shall stand erect, hold the ball at shoulder height and arm's length and drop it.

Dropped Ball Strikes Player or Equipment

If a ball when dropped, touches the player, his partner, either of their caddies, or their equipment, before or after it strikes the ground, the ball shall be re-dropped, without penalty.

Rule 20-3.
Placing and Replacing

a. By Whom and Where

A ball to be placed under the Rules shall be placed by the player or his partner. A ball to be replaced shall be replaced by the player, his partner or the person who lifted or moved it. In any such case, the player shall be responsible for any breach of the Rules.

If a ball or a ball-marker is accidentally moved in the process of placing or replacing the ball, no penalty is incurred and the ball or the ball-marker shall be replaced.

b. Lie of Ball to Be Placed or Replaced Altered

If the original lie of a ball to be placed or replaced has been altered:

(i)   except in a hazard, the ball shall be placed in the nearest lie most similar to the original lie which is not more than one club-length from the original lie, not nearer the hole and not in a hazard;

(ii)   in a water hazard, the ball shall be placed in accordance with Clause (i) above, except that the ball must be placed in the water hazard;

(iii) In a bunker, the original lie shall be recreated as nearly as possible and the ball shall be placed in that lie.

c. Spot Not Determinable

If it is impossible to determine the spot where the ball is to be placed:

(i)   through the green, the ball shall be dropped as near as possible to the place where it lay but not nearer the hole or in a hazard;

(ii)   In a hazard, the ball shall be dropped in the hazard as near as possible to the place where it lay but not nearer the hole;

(iii) on the putting green, the ball shall be placed as near as possible to the place where it lay but not nearer the hole or in a hazard.

Rule 20-3.
Placing and Replacing

d. Ball Fails to Remain on Spot

If a ball when placed fails to remain on the spot on which it was placed, it shall be replaced without penalty. If it still fails to remain on that spot:

(i) except in a <u>hazard,</u> it shall be placed at the nearest spot not nearer the hole or in a hazard where it can be placed at rest;

(ii) in a hazard, it shall be placed in the hazard at the nearest spot not nearer the hole where it can be placed at rest.

PENALTY FOR BREACH OF RULE 20-1, -2 or -3:
Match play — Loss of hole; Stroke play — Two strokes.

Will you mark your ball. It is going to be in my way.

Right, but first let's make sure we know what sort of lie I've got. If your shot alters my present lie I shall have to recreate the present lie as nearly as possible and place the ball in that lie. If it had happened on the fairway then I would have had to place my ball in the nearest most similar lie I could find, within one club-length, and not nearer the hole.

Even though I'm in a water hazard I'm going to play the ball as it lies. Your ball is going to be in my way. Would you mind marking it?

That's all right but there is one other proviso. You must place your ball in the hazard. (Rule 20-3b (ii)).

Not at all but let's note just what kind of a lie I have. If as a result of your shot my lie is altered I'm entitled to place my ball in the nearest lie most similar provided it's not more than one club-length away from the original lie and not nearer the hole.

If the player's ball in play has been lifted, it is again in play when dropped or placed.

A substituted ball becomes the ball in play if it is dropped or placed under an applicable Rule, whether or not such Rule permits substitution. A ball substituted under an inapplicable Rule is a wrong ball.

When, under the Rules, a player elects or is required to play his next stroke from where a previous stroke was played, he shall proceed as follows: if the stroke is to be played from the teeing ground, the ball to be played shall be played from anywhere within the teeing ground and may be teed; if the stroke is to be played from through the green or a hazard, it shall be dropped; if the stroke is to be played on the putting green, it shall be placed.

PENALTY FOR BREACH OF RULE 20-5:
Match play — Loss of hole; Stroke play — Two strokes.

A ball dropped or placed in a wrong place or otherwise not in accordance with the Rules but not played may be lifted, without penalty, and the player shall then proceed correctly.

For a ball played outside teeing ground, see Rule 11-4.

a. Match Play

If a player plays a stroke with a ball which has been dropped or placed in a wrong place, *he shall lose the hole.*

b. Stroke Play

If a competitor plays a stroke with (i) his original ball which has been dropped or placed in a wrong place, (ii) a substituted ball which has been dropped or placed under an applicable Rule but in a wrong place or (iii) his ball in play when it has been moved and not replaced in a case where the Rules require replacement, *he shall,* provided a serious breach has not occurred, *incur the penalty prescribed by the applicable Rule* and play out the hole with the ball.

If, after playing from a wrong place, a competitor becomes aware of that fact and believes that a serious breach may be involved, he may, provided he has not played a stroke from the next teeing ground or, in the case of the last hole of the round, left the putting green, declare that he will play out the hole with a second ball dropped or placed in accordance with the Rules. The competitor shall report the facts to the Committee before returning his score card; if he fails to do so, *he shall be disqualified.* The Committee shall determine whether a serious breach of the Rule occurred. If so, the score with the second ball shall count and *the competitor shall add two penalty strokes to his score with that ball.*

If a serious breach has occurred and the competitor has failed to correct it as prescribed above, *he shall be disqualified.*

Note: If a competitor plays a second ball, penalty strokes incurred by playing the ball ruled not to count and strokes subsequently taken with that ball shall be disregarded.

RULE 21.
Cleaning Ball

A ball on the putting green may be cleaned when lifted under Rule 16-1b. Elsewhere, a ball may be cleaned when lifted except when it has been lifted:

a. To determine if it is unfit for play (Rule 5-3);

b. For identification (Rule 12-2), in which case it may be cleaned only to the extent necessary for identification; or

c. Because it is interfering with or assisting play (Rule 22).

If a player cleans his ball during play of a hole except as provided in this Rule, *he shall incur a penalty of one stroke* and the ball, if lifted, shall be replaced.

If a player who is required to replace a ball fails to do so, *he shall incur the penalty* for breach of Rule 20-3a, but no additional penalty under Rule 21 shall be applied.

Exception: If a player incurs a penalty for failing to act in accordance with Rule 5-3, 12-2 or 22, no additional penalty under Rule 21 shall be applied.

RULE 22.
Ball Interfering with or Assisting Play

Any player may:

a. Lift his ball if he considers that it might assist any other player or

b. Have any other ball lifted if he considers that it might interfere with his play or assist the play of any other player,

but this may not be done while another ball is in motion. In stroke play, a player required to lift his ball may play first rather than lift. A ball lifted under this Rule shall be replaced.

If a ball is accidentally moved in complying with this Rule, no penalty is incurred and the ball shall be replaced.

PENALTY FOR BREACH OF RULE:
Match play — Loss of hole; Stroke play — Two strokes.

Definition

"Loose impediments" are natural objects such as stones, leaves, twigs, branches and the like, dung, worms and insects and casts or heaps made by them, provided they are not fixed or growing, are not solidly embedded and do not adhere to the ball.

Sand and loose soil are loose impediments on the <u>putting green</u> but not elsewhere.

Snow and ice are either <u>casual water</u> or loose impediments, at the option of the player, except that manufactured ice is an <u>obstruction.</u>

Dew is not a loose impediment.

Rule 23-1.
Relief

Except when both the <u>loose impediment</u> and the ball lie in or touch a <u>hazard</u>, any loose impediment may be removed without penalty. If the ball moves, see Rule 18-2c.

When a player's ball is in motion, a loose impediment on his line of play shall not be removed.

PENALTY FOR BREACH OF RULE:
Match play — Loss of hole; Stroke play — Two strokes.
(Searching for ball in hazard — see Rule 12-1.)
(Touching line of putt — see Rule 16-1a.)

Loose Impediments in a Hazard

The pine cone is a loose impediment and must not be touched in a hazard.
The tin is a movable obstruction and may be removed.

Obstructions

Definition

An "obstruction" is anything artificial, including the artificial surfaces and sides of roads and paths and manufactured ice, except:

a. Objects defining <u>out of bounds,</u> such as walls, fences, stakes and railings;

b. Any part of an immovable artificial object which is out of bounds; and

c. Any construction declared by the Committee to be an integral part of the course.

Rule 24-1.
Movable Obstruction

A player may obtain relief from a movable <u>obstruction</u> as follows:

a. If the ball does not lie in or on the obstruction, the obstruction may be removed; if the ball moves, no penalty is incurred and the ball shall be replaced.

b. If the ball lies in or on the obstruction, the ball may be lifted, without penalty, and the obstruction removed. The ball shall <u>through the green</u> or in a <u>hazard</u> be dropped, or on the <u>putting green</u> be placed, as near as possible to the spot directly under the place where the ball lay in or on the obstruction, but not nearer the hole.

The ball may be cleaned when lifted under Rule 24-1.

When a ball is in motion, an obstruction on the player's line of play other than an attended flagstick and equipment of the players shall not be removed.

Movable Obstruction: Ball Resting Against Rake Rolls Into Bunker

Rule 24-2.
Immovable Obstruction

a. Interference

Interference by an immovable <u>obstruction</u> occurs when a ball lies in or on the obstruction, or so close to the obstruction that the obstruction interferes with the player's <u>stance</u> or the area of his intended swing. If the player's ball lies on the <u>putting green</u>, interference also occurs if an immovable obstruction on the putting green intervenes on his line of putt. Otherwise, intervention on the line of play is not, of itself, interference under this Rule.

b. Relief

Except when the ball lies in or touches a <u>water hazard</u> or a <u>lateral water hazard</u>, a player may obtain relief from interference by an immovable <u>obstruction</u>, without penalty, as follows:

(i) **Through the Green:** if the ball lies <u>through the green</u>, the point on the <u>course</u> nearest to where the ball lies shall be determined (without crossing over, through or under the obstruction) which (a) is not nearer the hole, (b) avoids interference (as defined) and (c) is not in a <u>hazard</u> or on a <u>putting green</u>. The player shall lift the ball and drop it within one club-length of the point thus determined on ground which fulfils (a), (b) and (c) above.

Note: The prohibition against crossing over, through or under the <u>obstruction</u> does not apply to the artificial surfaces and sides of roads and paths or when the ball lies in or on the obstruction.

Continued

(ii) **In a Bunker:** If the ball lies in or touches a <u>bunker</u>, the player shall lift and drop the ball in accordance with Clause (i) above, except that the ball must be dropped in the bunker.

(iii) **On the Putting Green:** If the ball lies on the <u>putting green,</u> the player shall lift the ball and place it in the nearest position to where it lay which affords relief from interference, but not nearer the hole nor in a hazard.

The ball may be cleaned when lifted under Rule 24-2b.

(Ball rolling back into condition from which relief taken — see Rule 20-2c(v).)

Exception: A player may not obtain relief under Rule 24-2b if (a) it is clearly unreasonable for him to play a stroke because of interference by anything other than an immovable obstruction or (b) interference by an immovable obstruction would occur only through use of an unnecessarily abnormal stance, swing or direction of play.

Note: If a ball lies in or touches a <u>water hazard</u> (including a <u>lateral water hazard),</u> the player is not entitled to relief without penalty from interference by an immovable obstruction. The player shall play the ball as it lies or proceed under Rule 26-1.

PENALTY FOR BREACH OF RULE:
Match play — Loss of hole; Stroke play — Two strokes.

Immovable Obstruction

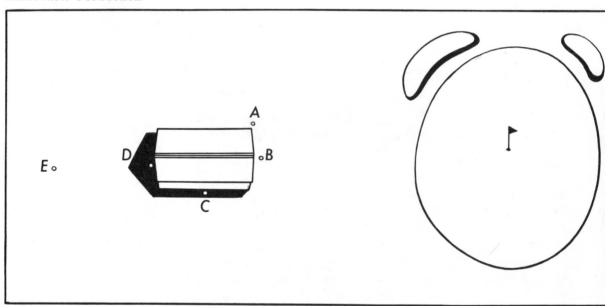

A—*Although the ball lies close to the shed (an obstruction) there is no interference with the player's stance or swing. So no relief.*

B—*Interference with player's backswing. Relief.*

C—*Interference with player's stance. Relief*

D—*Interference with player's swing (follow-through). Relief*

E—*While the shed intervenes between the ball and the hole, there is no interference with the player's stance or swing. So no relief.*

It has to be assumed in all these instances that the player is right-handed and intends to play directly at the flag.

Where relief is permitted the player should proceed under Rule 24-2b (i). In the case of D, intervention on the line of play is not, of itself, interference under this Rule.

Relief from Obstruction Gives Relief for Line of Play

No Relief Without Penalty in Water Hazard

Abnormal Ground Conditions and Wrong Putting Green

Definitions

"Casual water" is any temporary accumulation of water on the course which is visible before or after the player takes his stance and is not in a water hazard. Snow and ice are either casual water or loose impediments, at the option of the player, except that manufactured ice is an obstruction. Dew is not casual water.

"Ground under repair" is any portion of the course so marked by order of the Committee or so declared by its authorised representative. It includes material piled for removal and a hole made by a greenkeeper, even if not so marked. Stakes and lines defining ground under repair are in such ground. The margin of ground under repair extends vertically downwards, but not upwards.

Note 1: Grass cuttings and other material left on the course which have been abandoned and are not intended to be removed are not ground under repair unless so marked.

Note 2: The Committee may make a Local Rule prohibiting play from ground under repair.

Casual Water Out of Bounds

65

Grass Cuttings

Look at this. I'm going to take a free drop. These grass cuttings are ground under repair. What a bit of luck.

No. Those grass cuttings have obviously been thrown under that bush to rot away. They can't be said to be ground under repair unless the Committee has marked them as such. You'll either have to play the ball as it lies or declare it unplayable.

Ground Under Repair: Examples

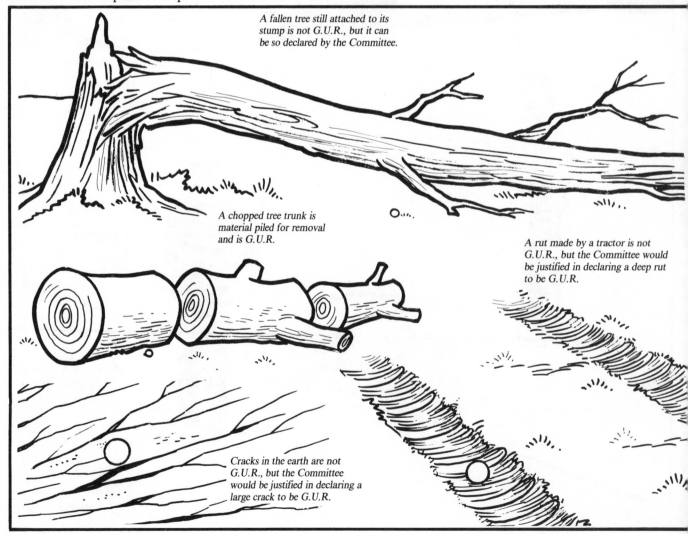

A fallen tree still attached to its stump is not G.U.R., but it can be so declared by the Committee.

A chopped tree trunk is material piled for removal and is G.U.R.

A rut made by a tractor is not G.U.R., but the Committee would be justified in declaring a deep rut to be G.U.R.

Cracks in the earth are not G.U.R., but the Committee would be justified in declaring a large crack to be G.U.R.

a. Interference

Interference by casual water, ground under repair or a hole, cast or runway made by a burrowing animal, a reptile or a bird occurs when a ball lies in or touches any of these conditions or when the condition interferes with the player's stance or the area of his intended swing.

If the player's ball lies on the putting green, interference also occurs if such condition on the putting green intervenes on his line of putt.

If interference exists, the player may either play the ball as it lies (unless prohibited by Local Rule) or take relief as provided in Clause b.

b. Relief

If the player elects to take relief, he shall proceed as follows:

(i) **Through the Green:** If the ball lies through the green, the point on the course nearest to where the ball lies shall be determined which (a) is not nearer the hole, (b) avoids interference by the condition, and (c) is not in a hazard or on a putting green. The player shall lift the ball and drop it without penalty within one club-length of the point thus determined on ground which fulfils (a), (b) and (c) above.

(ii) **In a Hazard:** If the ball lies in or touches a hazard, the player shall lift and drop the ball either:

(a) Without penalty, in the hazard, as near as possible to the spot where the ball lay, but not nearer the hole, on ground which affords maximum available relief from the condition; or

(b) *Under penalty of one stroke,* outside the hazard, keeping the point where the ball lay directly between the hole and the spot on which the ball is dropped.

Exception: If a ball lies in or touches a water hazard (including a lateral water hazard), the player is not entitled to relief without penalty from a hole, cast or runway made by a burrowing animal, a reptile or a bird. The player shall play the ball as it lies or proceed under Rule 26-1.

(iii) **On the Putting Green:** If the ball lies on the putting green, the player shall lift the ball and place it without penalty in the nearest position to where it lay which affords maximum available relief from the condition, but not nearer the hole nor in a hazard.

The ball may be cleaned when lifted under Rule 25-1b.

(Ball rolling back into condition from which relief taken — see Rule 20-2c(v).)

Exception: A player may not obtain relief under Rule 25-1b if (a) it is clearly unreasonable for him to play a stroke because of interference by anything other than a condition covered by Rule 25-1a or (b) interference by such a condition would occur only through use of an unnecessarily abnormal stance, swing or direction of play.

Continued

Casual Water. Place of Dropping Through the Green

Stance Interfered With by Burrowing Animal Hole: Ball Unplayable Because of Other Condition

c. Ball Lost Under Condition Covered by Rule 25-1.

It is a question of fact whether a ball lost after having been struck toward a condition covered by Rule 25-1 is lost under such condition. In order to treat the ball as lost under such condition, there must be reasonable evidence to that effect. In the absence of such evidence, the ball must be treated as a lost ball and Rule 27 applies.

(i) **Outside a Hazard** — If a ball is lost outside a hazard under a condition covered by Rule 25-1, the player may take relief as follows: the point on the course nearest to where the ball last crossed the margin of the area shall be determined which (a) is not nearer the hole than where the ball last crossed the margin, (b) avoids interference by the condition and (c) is not in a hazard or on a putting green. He shall drop a ball without penalty within one club-length of the point thus determined on ground which fulfils (a), (b) and (c) above.

(ii) **In a Hazard** — If a ball is lost in a hazard under a condition covered by Rule 25-1, the player may drop a ball either:
(a) Without penalty, in the hazard, as near as possible to the point at which the original ball last crossed the margin of the area, but not nearer the hole, on ground which affords maximum available relief from the condition;
or
(b) *Under penalty of one stroke,* outside the hazard, keeping the point at which the original ball last crossed the margin of the hazard directly between the hole and the spot on which the ball is dropped.

Exception: If a ball lies in a water hazard (including a lateral water hazard), the player is not entitled to relief without penalty for a ball lost in a hole, cast or runway made by a burrowing animal, a reptile or a bird. The player shall proceed under Rule 26-1.

Rule 25-2.
Embedded Ball

A ball embedded in its own pitch-mark in the ground in any closely mown area through the green may be lifted, cleaned and dropped, without penalty, as near as possible to the spot where it lay but not nearer the hole. "Closely mown area" means any area of the course, including paths through the rough, cut to fairway height or less.

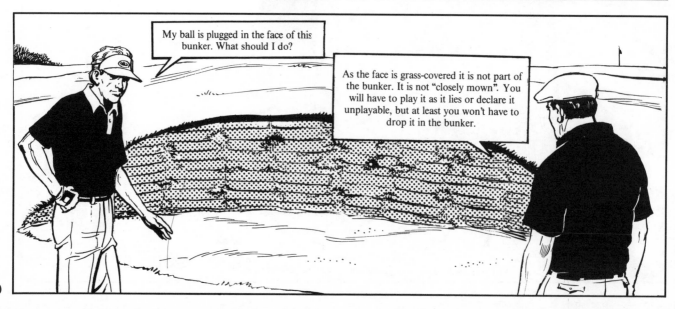

If a ball lies on a <u>putting green</u> other than that of the hole being played, the point on the <u>course</u> nearest to where the ball lies shall be determined which (a) is not nearer the hole and (b) is not in a <u>hazard</u> or on a putting green. The player shall lift the ball and drop it without penalty within one club-length of the point thus determined on ground which fulfils (a) and (b) above. The ball may be cleaned when so lifted.

Note: Unless otherwise prescribed by the Committee, the term "a putting green other than that of the hole being played" includes a practice putting green or pitching green on the course.

PENALTY FOR BREACH OF RULE:
Match play — Loss of hole; Stroke play — Two strokes.

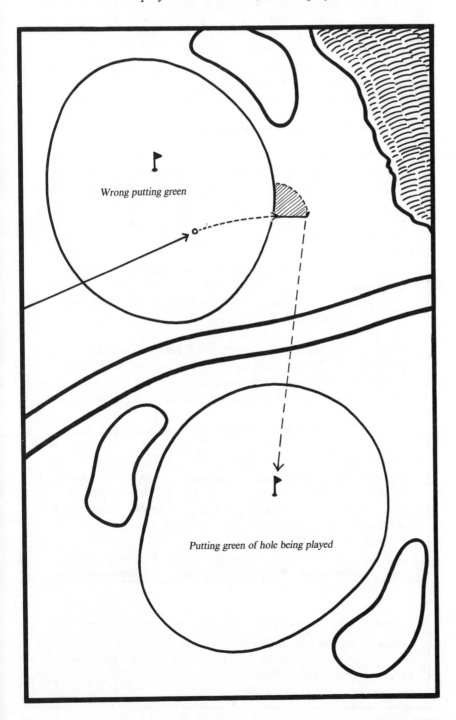

Wrong putting green

Putting green of hole being played

A ball lies on a wrong putting green and the point on the course nearest to which the ball lies which is not nearer the hole, is not in a hazard or on a putting green, is point A. The player must drop his ball within one club-length of point A (shaded area) not nearer the hole.

RULE 26.

Water Hazards

(Including Lateral Water Hazards)

Definitions

A "water hazard" is any sea, lake, pond, river, ditch, surface drainage ditch or other open water course (whether or not containing water) and anything of a similar nature.

All ground or water within the margin of a water hazard is part of the water hazard. The margin of a water hazard extends vertically upwards and downwards. Stakes and lines defining the margins of water hazards are in the hazards.

Note: Water hazards (other than <u>lateral water hazards</u>) should be defined by yellow stakes or lines.

A "lateral water hazard" is a <u>water hazard</u> or that part of a water hazard so situated that it is not possible or is deemed by the Committee to be impracticable to drop a ball behind the water hazard in accordance with Rule 26-1b.

That part of a water hazard to be played as a lateral water hazard should be distinctively marked.

Note: Lateral water hazards should be defined by red stakes or lines.

Rule 26-1.
Ball in Water Hazard

It is a question of fact whether a ball lost after having been struck towards a <u>water hazard</u> is lost inside or outside the hazard. In order to treat the ball as lost in the hazard, there must be reasonable evidence that the ball lodged in it. In the absence of such evidence, the ball must be treated as a lost ball and Rule 27 applies.

If a ball lies in, touches or is lost in a water hazard (whether the ball lies in water or not), the player may *under penalty of one stroke:*

a. Play his next stroke as nearly as possible at the spot from which the original ball was last played (see Rule 20-5);
or

b. Drop a ball behind the water hazard, keeping the point at which the original ball last crossed the margin of the water hazard directly between the hole and the spot on which the ball is dropped, with no limit to how far behind the water hazard the ball may be dropped;
or

c. *As additional options available only if the ball lies in, touches or is lost in a lateral water hazard,* drop a ball outside the water hazard within two club-lengths of (i) the point where the original ball last crossed the margin of the water hazard or (ii) a point on the opposite margin of the water hazard equidistant from the hole. The ball must be dropped and come to rest not nearer the hole than the point where the original ball last crossed the margin of the water hazard.

The ball may be cleaned when lifted under this Rule.

(Ball moving in water in a water hazard — see Rule 14-6.)

Rule 26-2.
Ball Played Within Water Hazard

a. Ball Comes to Rest in Hazard

If a ball played from within a water hazard comes to rest in the hazard after the stroke, the player may:

(i)   proceed under Rule 26-1; or

continued

(ii) *under penalty of one stroke*, play his next stroke as nearly as possible at the spot from which the last stroke from outside the hazard was played (see Rule 20-5).

b. Ball Lost or Unplayable Outside Hazard
or Out of Bounds

If a ball played from within a water hazard is lost or declared unplayable outside the hazard or is out of bounds, the player, after taking *a penalty of one stroke* under Rule 27-1 or 28a, may:

(i) play a ball as nearly as possible at the spot in the hazard from which the original ball was last played (see Rule 20-5); or

(ii) *under an additional penalty of one stroke*, proceed under Rule 26-1b or, if applicable, Rule 26-1c, using as the reference point the point where the original ball last crossed the margin of the hazard before it came to rest in the hazard; or

(iii) *under an additional penalty of one stroke*, play his next stroke as nearly as possible at the spot from which the last stroke from outside the hazard was played (see Rule 20-5).

Note: If a ball played from within a water hazard is declared unplayable outside the hazard, nothing in Rule 26-2b precludes the player from proceeding under Rule 28b or c.

PENALTY FOR BREACH OF RULE:
Match play — Loss of hole; Stroke play — Two strokes.

Ball Crossing Margin of Water Hazard

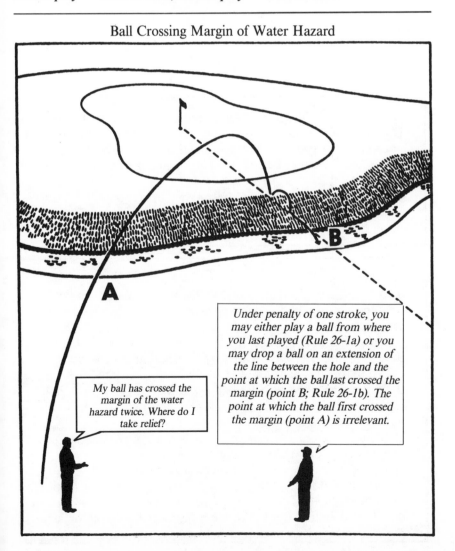

My ball has crossed the margin of the water hazard twice. Where do I take relief?

Under penalty of one stroke, you may either play a ball from where you last played (Rule 26-1a) or you may drop a ball on an extension of the line between the hole and the point at which the ball last crossed the margin (point B; Rule 26-1b). The point at which the ball first crossed the margin (point A) is irrelevant.

Ball Dropping Behind Water Margin

RULE 27.
Ball Lost or Out of Bounds;
Provisional Ball

If the original ball is lost under a condition covered by Rule 25-1 (casual water, ground under repair and certain damage to the course), the player may proceed under that Rule. If the original ball is lost in a water hazard, the player shall proceed under Rule 26.

Such Rules may not be used unless there is reasonable evidence that the ball is lost under a condition covered by Rule 25-1 or in a water hazard.

Definitions

A ball is "lost" if:

a. It is not found or identified as his by the player within five minutes after the player's side or his or their caddies have begun to search for it; or

b. The player has put another ball into play under the Rules, even though he may not have searched for the original ball; or

c. The player has played any stroke with a provisional ball from the place where the original ball is likely to be or from a point nearer the hole than that place, whereupon the provisional ball becomes the ball in play.

Time spent in playing a wrong ball is not counted in the five-minute period allowed for search.

"Out of bounds" is ground on which play is prohibited.

When out of bounds is defined by reference to stakes or a fence, or as being beyond stakes or a fence, the out of bounds line is determined by the nearest inside points of the stakes or fence posts at ground level excluding angled supports.

When out of bounds is defined by a line on the ground, the line itself is out of bounds.

The out of bounds line extends vertically upwards and downwards.

A ball is out of bounds when all of it lies out of bounds.

A player may stand out of bounds to play a ball lying within bounds.

A "provisional ball" is a ball played under Rule 27-2 for a ball which may be <u>lost</u> outside a <u>water hazard</u> or may be <u>out of bounds.</u>

Ball Found Within Five Minutes

Thanks for finding my ball. We hadn't been looking for it for five minutes, so I'll just play it.

Your ball wasn't "lost" merely because you went back to play another before the five minutes of search was up. But if you'd dropped or played another before I called you back that would have become the ball in play and this one would have been "lost", and you couldn't have played on with it.

Rule 27-1.
Ball Lost or Out of Bounds

If a ball is <u>lost</u> outside a <u>water hazard</u> or is <u>out of bounds</u>, the player shall play a ball, *under penalty of one stroke,* as nearly as possible at the spot from which the original ball was last played (see Rule 20-5).

PENALTY FOR BREACH OF RULE 27-1:
Match play — Loss of hole; Stroke play — Two strokes.

a. Procedure

If a ball may be <u>lost</u> outside a <u>water hazard</u> or may be <u>out of bounds</u>, to save time the player may play another ball provisionally as nearly as possible at the spot from which the original ball was played (see Rule 20-5). The player shall inform his opponent in match play or his marker or a fellow-competitor in stroke play that he intends to play a <u>provisional ball</u>, and he shall play it before he or his partner goes forward to search for the original ball. If he fails to do so and plays another ball, such ball is not a provisional ball and becomes the <u>ball in play</u> *under penalty of stroke and distance* (Rule 27-1); the original ball is deemed to be lost.

b. When Provisional Ball Becomes Ball in Play

The player may play a provisional ball until he reaches the place where the original ball is likely to be. If he plays a stroke with the provisional ball from the place where the original ball is likely to be or from a point nearer the hole than that place, the original ball is deemed to be <u>lost</u> and the provisional ball becomes the ball in play under *penalty of stroke and distance* (Rule 27-1).

If the original ball is lost outside a water hazard or is out of bounds, the provisional ball becomes the ball in play, *under penalty of stroke and distance* (Rule 27-1).

c. When Provisional Ball to Be Abandoned

If the original ball is neither lost outside a water hazard nor out of bounds, the player shall abandon the provisional ball and continue play with the original ball. If he fails to do so, any further strokes played with the provisional ball shall constitute playing a <u>wrong ball</u> and the provisions of Rule 15 shall apply.

Note: If the original ball lies in a water hazard, the player shall play the ball as it lies or proceed under Rule 26. If it is lost in a water hazard or unplayable, the player shall proceed under Rule 26 or 28, whichever is applicable.

Provisional Ball Becomes Ball in Play

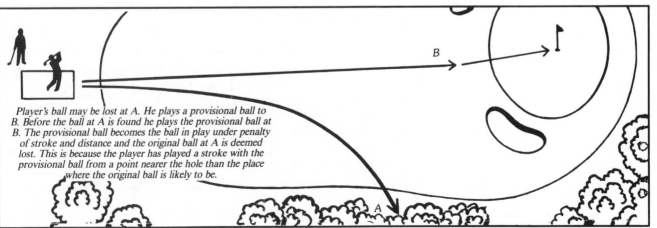

Player's ball may be lost at A. He plays a provisional ball to B. Before the ball at A is found he plays the provisional ball at B. The provisional ball becomes the ball in play under penalty of stroke and distance and the original ball at A is deemed lost. This is because the player has played a stroke with the provisional ball from a point nearer the hole than the place where the original ball is likely to be.

The ball may be lost in the bushes and the player plays a provisional ball. The original ball is found, but unplayable, within five minutes and before the provisional ball has become the ball in play. The player must abandon the provisional ball and proceed with the original ball, adopting one of the options under Rule 28.

RULE 28.
Ball Unplayable

The player may declare his ball unplayable at any place on the course except when the ball lies in or touches a water hazard. The player is the sole judge as to whether his ball is unplayable.
If the player deems his ball to be unplayable, he shall, *under penalty of one stroke:*
a. play his next stroke as nearly as possible at the spot from which the original ball was last played (see Rule 20-5);
or
b. Drop a ball within two club-lengths of the spot where the ball lay, but not nearer the hole;
or
c. Drop a ball behind the point where the ball lay, keeping that point directly between the hole and the spot on which the ball is dropped, with no limit to how far behind that point the ball may be dropped.
If the unplayable ball lies in a bunker and the player elects to proceed under Clause b or c, a ball must be dropped in the bunker.
The ball may be cleaned when lifted under this Rule.

PENALTY FOR BREACH OF RULE:
Match play — Loss of hole; Stroke play — Two strokes.

Ball unplayable in Bunker: Player's Options

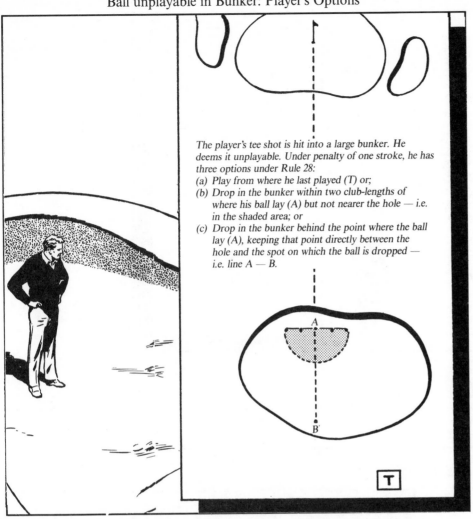

The player's tee shot is hit into a large bunker. He deems it unplayable. Under penalty of one stroke, he has three options under Rule 28:

(a) Play from where he last played (T) or;

(b) Drop in the bunker within two club-lengths of where his ball lay (A) but not nearer the hole — i.e. in the shaded area; or

(c) Drop in the bunker behind the point where the ball lay (A), keeping that point directly between the hole and the spot on which the ball is dropped — i.e. line A — B.

Ball unplayable in Bush: Place for Dropping

I'm going to declare that ball unplayable. I'm going to invoke option b and drop the ball within two club-lengths of where it is now lying.

That's O.K. But remember the ball when dropped must strike the ground within two club-lengths of where it lay.

OTHER FORMS OF PLAY

RULE 29.

Threesomes and Foursomes

Definitions

> Threesome: A match in which one plays against two, and each side plays one ball.
> Foursome: A match in which two play against two, and each side plays one ball.

Rule 29-1.
General

> In a threesome or a foursome, during any stipulated round the partners shall play alternately from the teeing grounds and alternately during the play of each hole. Penalty strokes do not affect the order of play.

Rule 29-2.
Match Play

> If a player plays when his partner should have played, *his side shall lose the hole.*

Rule 29-3.
Stroke Play

> If the partners play a stroke or strokes in incorrect order, such stroke or strokes shall be cancelled and *the side shall incur a penalty of two strokes.* The side shall correct the error by playing a ball in correct order at the spot from which it first played in incorrect order (see Rule 20-5). If the side plays a stroke from the next teeing ground without first correcting the error or, in the case of the last hole of the round, leaves the putting green without declaring its intention to correct the error, *the side shall be disqualified.*

RULE 30. Three-Ball,
Best-Ball and Four-Ball
Match Play

Definitions

Three-Ball: A match play competition in which three play against one another, each playing his own ball. Each player is playing two distinct matches.
Best-Ball: A match in which one plays against the better ball of two or the best ball of three players.
Four-Ball: A match in which two play their better ball against the better ball of two other players.

Rule 30-1.
Rules of Golf Apply

The Rules of Golf, so far as they are not at variance with the following special Rules, shall apply to three-ball, best-ball and four-ball matches.

Four-Ball. One Player May Represent Side

Breach of Rule by One Partner in Match Play

Your partner's late. Are you both disqualified, or just your partner?

Neither of us. As this is a four-ball match I'm entitled to represent the side. Let's start. My partner may join us later, at the conclusion of a hole.

Blast! I'm still in the bunker.

Yes partner. And I'm afraid you are disqualified for the hole. When you had that angry swing, after failing to get your ball out, you touched the sand with your club. Fortunately although I am in the same bunker I am not penalised, because your breach of the Rule did not assist my play.

a. Ball at Rest Moved by an Opponent

Except as otherwise provided in the Rules, if the player's ball is touched or moved by an opponent, his caddie or equipment other than during search, Rule 18-3b applies. *That opponent shall incur a penalty stroke in his match with the player,* but not in his match with the other opponent.

b. Ball Deflected or Stopped by an Opponent Accidentally

If a player's ball is accidentally deflected or stopped by an opponent, his caddie or equipment, no penalty shall be incurred. In his match with that opponent the player may play the ball as it lies or, before another stroke is played by either side, he may cancel the stroke and replay it (see Rule 20-5). In his match with the other opponent, the ball shall be played as it lies.

Exception: Ball striking person attending flagstick — see Rule 17-3b.

(Ball purposely deflected or stopped by an opponent — see Rule 1-2.)

Rule 30-2.
Three-Ball Match Play

A John, my ball has struck your trolley. What do I do now?

B In your match with me you may either play the ball as it lies or cancel that stroke and replay it.
   In your match with Jim you must play your original ball as it lies.

A That means I'm going to have two balls in play at the same time.

B That's right. Rule 30-2b.

Rule 30-3.
Best-Ball and Four-Ball Match Play

a. Representation of Side

A side may be represented by one partner for all or any part of a match; all partners need not be present. An absent partner may join a match between holes, but not during play of a hole.

b. Maximum of Fourteen Clubs

The side shall be penalised for a breach of Rule 4-4 by any partner.

c. Order of Play

Balls belonging to the same side may be played in the order the side considers best.

d. Wrong Ball

If a player plays a stroke with a wrong ball except in a hazard, *he shall be disqualified for that hole,* but his partner incurs no penalty even if the wrong ball belongs to him. The owner of the ball shall replace it on the spot from which it was played, without penalty. If the ball is not immediately recoverable, another ball may be substituted.

e. Disqualification of Side

(i) *A side shall be disqualified* for a breach of any of the following by any partner:

Rule 1-3 — Agreement to Waive Rules.
Rule 4-1,-2 or -3— Clubs.
Rule 5-1 or-2 — The Ball.
Rule 6-2a — Handicap (playing off higher handicap).
Rule 6-4 — Caddie.
Rule 6-7 — Undue Delay (repeated offence).
Rule 14-3 — Artificial Devices and Unusual Equipment.

(ii) *A side shall be disqualified* for a breach of any of the following by all partners:

Rule 6-3 — Time of Starting and Groups.
Rule 6-8 — Discontinuance of Play.   ***continued***

83

f. Effect of Other Penalties

If a player's breach of a Rule assists his partner's play or adversely affects an opponent's play, *the partner incurs the applicable penalty in addition to any penalty incurred by the player.*

In all other cases where a player incurs a penalty for breach of a Rule, the penalty shall not apply to his partner. Where the penalty is stated to be loss of hole, the effect shall be to disqualify the player for that hole.

g. Another Form of Match Play Concurrently

In a best-ball or four-ball match when another form of <u>match</u> play is played concurrently the above special Rules shall apply.

RULE 31.

Four-Ball Stroke Play

In four-ball stroke play two competitors play as partners, each playing his own ball. The lower score of the partners is the score for the hole. If one partner fails to complete the play of the hole, there is no penalty.

Rule 31-1.
Rules of Golf Apply

The Rules of Golf, so far as they are not at variance with the following special Rules, shall apply to four-ball stroke play.

Rule 31-2.
Representation of Side

A side may be represented by either partner for all or any part of a <u>stipulated round</u>; both partners need not be present. An absent competitor may join his partner between holes, but not during play of a hole.

Rule 31-3.
Maximum of Fourteen Clubs

The side shall be penalised for a breach of Rule 4-4 by either partner.

Rule 31-4.
Scoring

The marker is required to record for each hole only the gross score of whichever partner's score is to count. The gross scores to count must be individually identifiable; otherwise *the side shall be disqualified.* Only one of the partners need be responsible for complying with Rule 6-6b.
(Wrong score — see Rule 31-7a.)

Rule 31-5.
Order of Play

Balls belonging to the same side may be played in the order the side considers best.

Date 6th June 1988
Competition OPEN FOUR-BALL

(S.S.S. 70)

PLAYER A J. JONES   Handicap 18   Strokes 18
PLAYER B R. SMITH   Handicap 12   Strokes 12

Hole	Length Yards	Par	Stroke Index	Gross Score A	Gross Score B	Nett Score A	Nett Score B	Won/Lost/Half	Max Score
1	437	4	4		5		4		4
2	320	4	14		4		(3)		4
3	162	3	18		4		4		4
4	504	5	7	6		5			5
5	181	3	16	4		3			4
6	443	4	2		5		4		4
7	390	4	8	5		4			3
8	346	4	12	5		4			4
9	340	4	10	4			3		4
Out	3123	35				34	5		36

Player's Signature _J. Jones_
Marker's Signature _H. Marshall_

Hole	Length Yards	Par	Stroke Index	Gross Score A	Gross Score B	Nett Score A	Nett Score B	Won/Lost/Half	Max Score
10	425	4	3		5		4		5
11	141	3	17	3		2			3
12	476	5	9	6		5			5
13	211	3	11	4	4		3		4
14	437	4	5		5		4		4
15	460	4	1		5		4		4
16	176	3	15	4		3			2
17	340	4	13		4		4		4
18	435	4	6	6		5			4
In	3101	34				34			36
Out	3123	35				34	5		35
Ttl	6224	69				6	89		71
Handicap									
Net Score									
Result									

(1) The lower score of the partners is the score for the hole (Rule 31).

(2) Only one of the partners need be responsible for complying with Rule 6-6b, i.e. recording scores, checking scores, countersigning and returning the card (Rule 31-4).

(3) The competitor is solely responsible for the correctness of the gross score recorded. Although there is no objection to the competitor (or his marker) entering the net score, it is the Committee's responsibility to record the better ball score for each hole, to add up the scores and to apply the handicaps recorded on the card (Rule 33-5). Thus there is no penalty for the error in recording the net score at the second hole.

(4) Scores of the two partners must be kept in seperate columns otherwise it is impossible for the Committee to apply the correct handicap. If the scores of both partners, having different handicaps, are recorded in the same column, the Committee has no alternative but to disqualify both partners. (Rules 31-7 and 6-6 apply).

(5) There is nothing in the Rules that requires an alteration to be initialled.

(6) The Committee is responsible for laying down the conditions under which a competition is to be played (Rule 33-1), including the method of handicapping.

In the above illustration the Committee laid down that full handicaps would apply.

**Rule 31-6.
Wrong Ball**

If a competitor plays a stroke with a <u>wrong ball</u> except in a <u>hazard</u>, *he shall add two penalty strokes to his score for the hole* and shall then play the correct ball. His partner incurs no penalty even if the wrong ball belongs to him.

The owner of the ball shall replace it on the spot from which it was played, without penalty. If the ball is not immediately recoverable, another ball may be substituted.

**Rule 31-7.
Disqualification Penalties**

a. Breach by One Partner
A side shall be disqualified from the competition for a breach of any of the following by either partner:

Rule 1-3 —	Agreement to Waive Rules.
Rule 3-4 —	Refusal to Comply with Rule.
Rule 4-1,-2 or-3—	Clubs.
Rule 5-1 or-2 —	The Ball.
Rule 6-2b —	Handicap (playing off higher handicap; failure to record handicap).
Rule 6-4 —	Caddie.
Rule 6-6b —	Signing and Returning Card.
Rule 6-6d —	Wrong Score for Hole, i.e. when the recorded lower score of the partners is lower than actually taken. If the recorded lower score of the partners is higher than actually taken, it must stand as returned.
Rule 6-7 —	Undue Delay (repeated offence).
Rule 7-1 —	Practice Before or Between Rounds.
Rule 14-3 —	Artificial Devices and Unusual Equipment.
Rule 31-4 —	Gross Scores to count Not Individually Identifiable.

b. Breach by Both Partners
A side shall be disqualified:
(i)   for a breach by both partners of Rule 6-3 (Time of Starting and Groups) or Rule 6-8 (Discontinuance of Play), or
(ii) if, at the same hole, each partner is in breach of a Rule the penalty for which is disqualification from the competition or for a hole.

c. For the Hole Only
In all other cases where a breach of a Rule would entail disqualification, *the competitor shall be disqualified only for the hole at which the breach occurred.*

**Rule 31-8.
Effect of Other Penalties**

If a competitor's breach of a Rule assists his partner's play, *the partner incurs the applicable penalty in addition to any penalty incurred by the competitor.*

In all other cases where a competitor incurs a penalty for breach of a Rule, the penalty shall not apply to his partner.

RULE 32. Bogey, Par and Stableford Competitions

Bogey, par and Stableford competitions are forms of stroke competition in which play is against a fixed score at each hole. The Rules for stroke play, so far as they are not at variance with the following special Rules, apply.

a. Bogey and Par Competitions

The reckoning for bogey and par competitions is made as in match play. Any hole for which a competitor makes no return shall be regarded as a loss. The winner is the competitor who is most successful in the aggregate of holes.

The marker is responsible for marking only the gross number of strokes for each hole where the competitor makes a net score equal to or less than the fixed score.

Note: Maximum of 14 Clubs — Penalties as in match play — see Rule 4-4.

b. Stableford Competitions

The reckoning in Stableford competitions is made by points awarded in relation to a fixed score at each hole as follows:

Hole Played in	Points
More than one over fixed score or no score returned	0
One over fixed score	1
Fixed Score	2
One under fixed score	3
Two under fixed score	4
Three under fixed score	5

The winner is the competitor who scores the highest number of points.

The marker shall be responsible for marking only the gross number of strokes at each hole where the competitor's net score earns one or more points.

Note: Maximum of 14 Clubs (Rule 4-4) — Penalties applied as follows: From total points scored for the round, deduction of two points for each hole at which any breach occurred; maximum deduction per round: four points.

a. From the Competition

A competitor shall be disqualified from the competition for a breach of any of the following:

Rule 1-3 —	Agreement to Waive Rules.
Rule 3-4 —	Refusal to Comply with Rule.
Rule 4-1,-2 or-3—	Clubs.
Rule 5-1 or -2 —	The Ball.
Rule 6-2b —	Handicap (playing off higher handicap; failure to record handicap).
Rule 6-3 —	Time of Starting and Groups.
Rule 6-4 —	Caddie.
Rule 6-6b —	Signing and Returning Card.
Rule 6-6d —	Wrong Score for Hole, except that no penalty shall be incurred when a breach of this Rule does not affect the result of the hole.
Rule 6-7 —	Undue Delay (repeated offence).
Rule 6-8 —	Discontinuance of Play.
Rule 7-1 —	Practice Before or Between Rounds.
Rule 14-3 —	Artificial Devices and Unusual Equipment.

b. For a Hole

In all other cases where a breach of a Rule would entail disqualification, *the competitor shall be disqualified only for the hole at which the breach occurred.*

RULE 33. The Committee

Rule 33-1.
Conditions; Waiving Rule

The Committee shall lay down the conditions under which a competition is to be played.

The Committee has no power to waive a Rule of Golf.

Certain special rules governing stroke play are so substantially different from those governing match play that combining the two forms of play is not practicable and is not permitted. The results of matches played and the scores returned in these circumstances shall not be accepted.

In stroke play the Committee may limit a referee's duties.

Rule 33-2.
The Course

a. Defining Bounds and Margins

The Committee shall define accurately:

(i)   the <u>course</u> and <u>out of bounds</u>,
(ii) the margins of <u>water hazards</u> and <u>lateral water hazards</u>,
(iii) <u>ground under repair</u>, and
(iv) <u>obstructions</u> and integral parts of the course.

b. New Holes

New holes should be made on the day on which a stroke competition begins and at such other times as the Committee considers necessary, provided all competitors in a single round play with each hole cut in the same position.

Exception: When it is impossible for a damaged hole to be repaired so that it conforms with the Definition, the Committee may make a new hole in a nearby similar position.

c. Practice Ground

Where there is no practice ground available outside the area of a competition <u>course</u>, the Committee should lay down the area on which players may practise on any day of a competition, if it is practicable to do so. On any day of a stroke competition, the Committee should not normally permit practice on or to a <u>putting green</u> or from a <u>hazard</u> of the competition course.

d. Course Unplayable

If the Committee or its authorised representative considers that for any reason the course is not in a playable condition, or that there are circumstances which render the proper playing of the game impossible, it may, in match play or stroke play, order a temporary suspension of play or, in stroke play, declare play null and void and cancel all scores for the round in question. When play has been temporarily suspended, it shall be resumed from where it was discontinued, even though resumption occurs on a subsequent day. When a round is cancelled, all penalties incurred in that round are cancelled.

(Procedure in discontinuing play — see Rule 6-8.)

The Committee shall lay down the times of starting and, in stroke play, arrange the groups in which competitors shall play.

When a match play competition is played over an extended period, the Committee shall lay down the limit of time within which each round shall be completed. When players are allowed to arrange the date of their match within these limits, the Committee should announce that the match must be played at a stated time on the last day of the period unless the players agree to a prior date.

Rule 33-3.
Times of Starting and Groups

The Committee shall publish a table indicating the order of holes at which handicap strokes are to be given or received.

Rule 33-4.
Handicap Stroke Table

In stroke play, the Committee shall issue for each competitor a score card containing the date and the competitor's name or, in foursome or four-ball stroke play, the competitors' names.

In stroke play, the Committee is responsible for the addition of scores and application of the handicap recorded on the card.

In four-ball stroke play, the Committee is responsible for recording the better-ball score for each hole and in the process applying the handicaps recorded on the card, and adding the better-ball scores.

In bogey, par and Stableford competitions, the Committee is responsible for applying the handicap recorded on the card and determining the result of each hole and the overall result or points total.

Rule 33-5.
Score Card

The Committee shall announce the manner, day and time for the decision of a halved match or of a tie, whether played on level terms or under handicap.

A halved match shall not be decided by stroke play. A tie in stroke play shall not be decided by a match.

Rule 33-6.
Decision of Ties

A penalty of disqualification may in exceptional individual cases be waived, modified or imposed if the Committee considers such action warranted.

Rule 33-7.
Disqualification Penalty;
Committee Discretion

a. Policy
The Committee may make and publish Local Rules for abnormal conditions if they are consistent with the policy of the Governing Authority for the country concerned as set forth in Appendix I to these Rules.

b. Waiving Penalty
A penalty imposed by a Rule of Golf shall not be waived by a Local Rule.

Rule 33-8.
Local Rules

RULE 34.

Disputes and Decisions

Rule 34-1.
Claims and Penalties

a. Match Play
In match play if a claim is lodged with the Committee under Rule 2-5, a decision should be given as soon as possible so that the state of the match may, if necessary, be adjusted.

If a claim is not made within the time limit provided by Rule 2-5, it shall not be considered unless it is based on facts previously unknown to the player making the claim and the player making the claim had been given wrong information (Rules 6-2a and 9) by an opponent. In any case, no later claim shall be considered after the result of the match has been officially announced, unless the Committee is satisfied that the opponent knew he was giving wrong information.

b. Stroke Play
Except as provided below, in stroke play no penalty shall be rescinded, modified or imposed after the competition is closed. A competition is deemed to have closed when the result has been officially announced or, in stroke play qualifying followed by match play, when the player has teed off in his first match.

A penalty of disqualification shall be imposed at any time if a competitor:

(i)   returns a score for any hole lower than actually taken (Rule 6-6d) for any reason other than failure to include a penalty which he did not know he had incurred; or

(ii)   returns a score card on which he has recorded a handicap which he knows is higher than that to which he is entitled, and this affects the number of strokes received (Rule 6-2b).

Rule 34-2.
Referee's Decision

If a referee has been appointed by the Committee, his decision shall be final.

Rule 34-3.
Committee's Decision

In the absence of a referee, the players shall refer any dispute to the Committee, whose decision shall be final.

If the Committee cannot come to a decision, it shall refer the dispute to the Rules of Golf Committee of the Royal and Ancient Golf Club of St. Andrews, whose decision shall be final.

If the point in doubt or dispute has not been referred to the Rules of Golf Committee, the player or players have the right to refer an agreed statement through the Secretary of the Club to the Rules of Golf Committee for an opinion as to the correctness of the decision given. The reply will be sent to the Secretary of the Club or Clubs concerned.

If play is conducted other than in accordance with the Rules of Golf, the Rules of Golf Committee will not give a decision on any question.

The Committee may make and publish Local Rules (for Specimen Local Rules see Part B) for such abnormal conditions as:

1. Obstructions

a. General

Clarifying the status of objects which may be obstructions (Rule 24).

Declaring any construction to be an integral part of the course and, accordingly, not an obstruction, e.g. built-up sides of teeing grounds, putting greens and bunkers (Rules 24 and 33-2a).

b. Stones in Bunkers.

Allowing the removal of stones in bunkers by declaring them to be "movable obstructions" (Rule 24).

c. Roads and Paths

(i) Declaring artificial surfaces and sides of roads and paths to be integral parts of the course, or

(ii) Providing relief of the type afforded under Rule 24-2b from roads and paths not having artificial surfaces and sides if they could unfairly affect play.

d. Fixed Sprinkler Heads

Providing relief from intervention by fixed sprinkler heads within two club-lengths of the putting green when the ball lies within two club-lengths of the sprinkler head.

e. Temporary Immovable Obstructions

Specimen Local Rules for application in Tournament Play are available from the Royal and Ancient Golf Club of St. Andrews.

2. Areas of the Course Requiring Preservation

Assisting preservation of the course by defining areas, including turf nurseries, young plantations and other parts of the course under cultivation, as "ground under repair" from which play is prohibited.

3. Unusual Damage to the Course or Accumulation of Leaves (or the like)

Declaring such areas to be "ground under repair" (Rule 25).

Note: For relief from aerification holes see Specimen Local Rule 7 in Part B of this Appendix.

4. Extreme Wetness, Mud, Poor Conditions and Protection of Course

a. Lifting an Embedded Ball, Cleaning

Where the ground is unusually soft, the Committee may, by temporary Local Rule, allow the lifting of a ball which is embedded in its own pitch-mark in the ground in an area "through the green" which is not "closely mown" (Rule 25-2) if it is satisfied that the proper playing of the game would otherwise be prevented. The Local Rule shall be for that day only or for a short period, and if practicable shall be confined to specified areas. The Committee shall withdraw the Local Rule as soon as conditions warrant and should not print it on the score card.

continued

In similarly adverse conditions, the Committee may, by temporary Local Rule, permit the cleaning of a ball "through the green".

b. "Preferred Lies" and "Winter Rules"

Adverse conditions, including the poor condition of the course or the existence of mud, are sometimes so general, particularly during winter months, that the Committee may decide to grant relief by temporary Local Rule either to protect the course or to promote fair and pleasant play. Such Local Rule shall be withdrawn as soon as conditions warrant.

5. Other Local Conditions which Interfere with the Proper Playing of the Game

If this necessitates modification of a Rule of Golf the approval of the Governing Authority must be obtained.

Other matters which the Committee could cover by Local Rule include:

6. Water Hazards

a. Lateral Water Hazards

Clarifying the status of sections of water hazards which may be lateral water hazards (Rule 26).

b. Provisional Ball

Permitting play of a provisional ball for a ball which may be in a water hazard of such character that it would be impracticable to determine whether the ball is in the hazard or to do so would unduly delay play. In such a case, if a provisional ball is played and the original ball is in a water hazard, the player may play the original ball as it lies or continue the provisional ball in play, but he may not proceed under Rule 26-1.

7. Defining Bounds and Margins

Specifying means used to define out of bounds, hazards, water hazards, lateral water hazards and ground under repair.

8. Dropping Zones

Establishing special areas in which balls may or shall be dropped when it is not feasible or practicable to proceed exactly in conformity with Rule 24-2b (Immovable Obstruction), Rule 25-1b or Rule 25-1c (Ground Under Repair), Rule 26-1 (Water Hazards and Lateral Water Hazards) or Rule 28 (Ball Unplayable).

9. Priority on the Course

The Committee may make regulations governing Priority on the Course (see Etiquette).

Part B – Specimen Local Rules

Within the policy set out in Part A of this Appendix the Committee may adopt a Specimen Local Rule by referring, on a score card or notice board, to the examples given below. However Specimen Local Rules 4, 5 or 6 should not be printed or referred to on a score card as they are all of limited duration.

1. Fixed Sprinkler Heads

All fixed sprinkler heads are immovable obstructions and relief from interference by them may be obtained under Rule 24-2. In addition, if such an obstruction on or within two club-lengths of the putting green of the hole being played intervenes on the line of play between the ball and the hole, the player may obtain relief,

continued

without penalty, as follows:

If the ball lies off the putting green but not in a hazard and is within two club-lengths of the intervening obstruction, it may be lifted, cleaned and dropped at the nearest point to where the ball lay which (a) is not nearer the hole, (b) avoids such intervention and (c) is not in a hazard or on a putting green.

PENALTY FOR BREACH OF LOCAL RULE:
Match play — Loss of hole; Stroke play — Two strokes.

2. Stones in Bunkers

Stones in bunkers are movable obstructions. Rule 24-1 applies.

3. Ground Under Repair: Play Prohibited

If a player's ball lies in an area of "ground under repair" from which play is prohibited, or if such an area of "ground under repair" interferes with the player's stance or the area of his intended swing the player must take relief under Rule 25-1.

PENALTY FOR BREACH OF LOCAL RULE:
Match play — Loss of hole; Stroke play — Two strokes.

4. Lifting an Embedded Ball

(Specify the area if practicable) .... through the green, a ball embedded in its own pitch-mark in ground other than sand may be lifted, cleaned and dropped, without penalty, as near as possible to the spot where it lay but not nearer the hole.

PENALTY FOR BREACH OF LOCAL RULE:
Match play — Loss of hole; Stroke play — Two strokes.

5. Cleaning Ball

(Specify the area if practicable) .... through the green a ball may be lifted, cleaned and replaced without penalty.

Note: The position of the ball shall be marked before it is lifted under this Local Rule — see Rule 20-1.

6. "Preferred Lies" and "Winter Rules"

A ball lying on any "closely mown area" through the green may, without penalty, be moved or may be lifted, cleaned and placed within six inches of where it originally lay, but not nearer the hole. After the ball has been so moved or placed, it is in play.

PENALTY FOR BREACH OF LOCAL RULE:
Match play — Loss of hole; Stroke play — Two strokes.

7. Aerification Holes

If a ball comes to rest in an aerification hole, the player may, without penalty, lift the ball and clean it. Through the green, the player shall drop the ball as near as possible to where it lay, but not nearer the hole. On the putting green, the player shall place the ball at the nearest spot not nearer the hole which avoids such situation.

PENALTY FOR BREACH OF LOCAL RULE:
Match play — Loss of hole; Stroke play — Two strokes.

Rule 33-1 provides, "The Committee shall lay down the conditions under which a competition is to be played". Such conditions should include many matters such as method of entry, eligibility, number of rounds to be played, settling ties, etc. which it is not appropriate to deal with in the Rules of Golf or this Appendix.

However there are four matters which might be covered in the Conditions of the Competition to which the Committee's attention is specifically drawn by way of a Note to the appropriate Rule. These are:

1. Specification of the Ball (Note to Rule 5-1)

Arising from the regulations for ball-testing under Rule 5-1, Lists of Conforming Golf Balls will be issued from time to time.

It is recommended that the Lists should be applied to all National and County (or equivalent) Championships and to all top class events when restricted to low handicap players. In order to apply the Lists to a particular competition the Committee must lay this down in the Conditions of the Competition. This should be referred to in the Entry Form, and also a notice should be displayed on the Club notice board and at the 1st Tee along the following lines:

.... (Name of Event) ....
.... (Date and Club) ....

The ball the player uses shall be named on the current List of Conforming Golf Balls issued by the Royal and Ancient Golf Club of St. Andrews.

Note 1: A penalty statement will be required and must be either:

(a) "PENALTY FOR BREACH OF CONDITION:
Disqualification".

or

(b) "PENALTY FOR BREACH OF CONDITION:

Match play — Loss of each hole at which a breach occurred: Stroke play — Two strokes for each hole at which a breach occurred".

If option (b) is adopted this only applies to use of a ball which, whilst not on the List of Conforming Golf Balls, does conform to the specifications set forth in Rule 5 and Appendix III. The penalty for use of a ball which does not so conform is disqualification.

Note 2: In Club events it is recommended that no such condition be applied.

2. Time of Starting (Note to Rule 6-3a)

If the Committee wishes to act in accordance with the Note, the following wording is recommended:

"If, in the absence of circumstances which warrant waiving the penalty of disqualification as provided in Rule 33-7, the player arrives at his starting point, ready to play, within five minutes after his starting time, the penalty for failure to start on time is loss of the first hole in match play or two strokes at the first hole in stroke play."

continued

3. Practice
The Committee may make regulations governing practice in accordance with the Note to Rule 7-1, Exception (c) to Rule 7-2, Note 2 to Rule 7 and Rule 33-2c.

4. Advice in Team Competitions
If the Committee wishes to act in accordance with the Note, the following wording is recommended:

"In accordance with the Note to Rule 8-1 of the Rules of Golf each team may appoint one person (in addition to the persons from whom advice may be asked under that Rule) who may give advice to members of that team. Such person [*if it is desired to insert any restriction on who may be nominated insert such restriction here*] shall be identified to the Committee prior to the start of the competition."

APPENDICES II AND III

Any design in a club or ball which is not covered by Rules 4 and 5 and Appendices II and III, or which might significantly change the nature of the game, will be ruled on by the Royal and Ancient Golf Club of St. Andrews and the United States Golf Association.

Note: Equipment approved for use or marketed prior to January 1st, 1984 which conformed to the Rules in effect in 1983 but does not conform to the 1984 Rules may be used until December 31st, 1989; thereafter all equipment must conform to the current Rules.

APPENDIX II

Design of Clubs

Rule 4-1 prescribes general regulations for the design of clubs. The following paragraphs, which provide some detailed specifications and clarify how Rule 4-1 is interpreted, should be read in conjunction with this Rule.

Rule 4-1b. Shaft

Generally Straight. The shaft shall be at least 18 inches (457mm) in length. It shall be straight from the top of the grip to a point not more than 5 inches (127mm) above the sole, measured along the axis of the shaft and the neck or socket.

Bending and Twisting Properties. The shaft must be so designed and manufactured that at any point along its length:
(i)   it bends in such a way that the deflection is the same regardless of how the shaft is rotated about its longitudinal axis; and
(ii) it twists the same amount in both directions.

Attachment to Clubhead. The neck or socket must not be more than 5 inches (127mm) in length, measured from the top of the neck or socket to the sole along its axis. The shaft and the neck or

continued

socket must remain in line with the heel, or with a point to the right or left of the heel, when the club is viewed in the address position. The distance between the axis of the shaft or the neck or socket and the back of the heel must not exceed 0.625 inches (16mm).

Exception for Putters: The shaft or neck or socket of a putter may be fixed at any point in the head and need not remain in line with the heel. The axis of the shaft from the top to a point not more than 5 inches (127mm) above the sole must diverge from the vertical in the toe-heel plane by at least 10 degrees when the club is in its normal address position.

Rule 4-1c. Grip

(i)   For clubs other than putters the grip must be generally circular in cross-section, except that a continuous, straight, slightly raised rib may be incorporated along the full length of the grip.

(ii) A putter grip may have a non-circular cross-section, provided the cross-section has no concavity and remains generally similar throughout the length of the grip.

(iii) The grip may be tapered but must not have any bulge or waist.

(iv) For clubs other than putters the axis of the grip must coincide with the axis of the shaft.

Rule 4-1d. Clubhead

Dimensions. The dimensions of a clubhead (see diagram) are measured, with the clubhead in its normal address position, on horizontal lines between vertical projections of the outermost points of (i) the heel and the toe and (ii) the face and the back. If the outermost point of the heel is not clearly defined, it is deemed to be 0.625 inches (16mm) above the horizontal plane on which the club is resting in its normal address position.

Plain in Shape. The clubhead shall be generally plain in shape. All parts shall be rigid, structural in nature and functional.

Features such as holes through the head, windows or transparencies, or appendages to the main body of the head such as plates, rods or fins for the purpose of meeting dimensional specifications, for aiming or for any other purpose are not permitted. Exceptions may be made for putters.

Any furrows in or runners on the sole shall not extend into the face.

Rule 4-1e. Club Face

Hardness and Rigidity. The club face must not be designed and manufactured to have the effect at impact of a spring which would unduly influence the movement of the ball.

Markings. Except for specified markings, the surface roughness must not exceed that of decorative sandblasting. Markings must not have sharp edges or raised lips, as determined by a finger test. Markings within the area where impact is intended (the "impact area") are governed by the following:

continued

(i) **Grooves.** A series of straight grooves with diverging sides and a symmetrical cross-section may be used. (See diagram.) The width and cross-section must be generally consistent across the face of the club and along the length of the grooves. Any rounding of groove edges shall be in the form of a radius which does not exceed 0.020 inches (0.5mm). The width of the grooves shall not exceed 0.035 inches (0.9mm), using the 30 degree method of measurement on file with the Royal and Ancient Golf Club of St. Andrews. The distance between edges of adjacent grooves must not be less than three times the width of a groove, and not less than 0.075 inches (1.9mm). The depth of a groove must not exceed 0.020 inches (0.5mm).

(ii) **Punch Marks.** Punch marks may be used. The area of any such mark must not exceed 0.0044 square inches (2.8 sq.mm). A mark must not be closer to an adjacent mark than 0.168 inches (4.3mm) measured from centre to centre. The depth of a punch mark must not exceed 0.040 inches (1.0mm). If punch marks are used in combination with grooves, a punch mark may not be closer to a groove than 0.168 inches (4.3mm), measured from centre to centre.

Decorative Markings. The centre of the impact area may be indicated by a design within the boundary of a square whose sides are 0.375 inches (9.5mm) in length. Such a design must not unduly influence the movement of the ball. Markings outside the impact area must not be greater than 0.040 inches (1.00mm) in depth and width.

Non-metallic Club Face Markings. The above specifications for markings do not apply to non-metallic clubs with loft angles less than 24 degrees, but markings which could unduly influence the movement of the ball are prohibited. Non-metallic clubs with a loft or face angle exceeding 24 degrees may have grooves of maximum width 0.040 inches (1.0mm) and maximum depth 1½ times the groove width, but must otherwise conform to the markings specifications above.

a. Weight
The weight of the ball shall not be greater than 1.620 ounces avoirdupois (45.93gm).

b. Size
The diameter of the ball shall be not less than 1.680 inches (42.67mm). This specification will be satisfied if, under its own weight, a ball falls through a 1.680 inches diameter ring gauge in fewer than 25 out of 100 randomly selected positions, the test being carried out at a temperature of 23 ± 1°C.

continued

c. Spherical Symmetry

The ball shall be designed and manufactured to perform in general as if it were spherically symmetrical.

As outlined in procedures on file at the Royal and Ancient Golf Club of St. Andrews, differences in peak angle of trajectory, carry and time of flight will be measured when 40 balls of the same type are launched, spinning 20 about one axis and 20 about another axis.

These tests will be performed using apparatus approved by the Royal and Ancient Golf Club of St. Andrews. If in two successive tests differences in the same two or more measurements are statistically significant at the 5% level of significance and exceed the limits set forth below, the ball type will not conform to the symmetry specification.

Measurement	Maximum Absolute Difference of the Means
Peak angle of trajectory	0.9 grid units (approx. 0.4 degrees)
Carry distance	2.5 yards
Flight time	0.16 seconds

Note: Methods of determining whether a ball performs as if it were generally spherically symmetrical may be subject to change as instrumentation becomes available to measure other properties accurately, such as the aerodynamic coefficient of lift, coefficient of drag and moment of inertia.

d. Initial Velocity

The velocity of the ball shall not be greater than 250 feet (76.2m) per second when measured on apparatus approved by the Royal and Ancient Golf Club of St. Andrews. A maximum tolerance of 2% will be allowed. The temperature of the ball when tested shall be $23 \pm 1^{\circ}C$.

e. Overall Distance Standard

A brand of golf ball, when tested on apparatus approved by the Royal and Ancient Golf Club of St. Andrews under the conditions set forth in the Overall Distance Standard for golf balls on file with the Royal and Ancient Golf Club of St Andrews, shall not cover an average distance in carry and roll exceeding 280 yards (256 metres) plus a tolerance of 6%.

Note: The 6% tolerance will be reduced to a minimum of 4% as test techniques are improved.

Notes to Appendix III

1: The size specification in (b) above will take effect from 1st January, 1990. Until that date the previous size specification of a diameter not less that 1.620 inches (41.15mm) will apply.

2: The Overall Distance Standard will apply only to balls which meet the new size specification of a diameter not less than 1.680 inches (42.67mm).

3: In international team competitions, until 31st December, 1989, the previous size specification of a diameter not less than 1.620 inches (41.15mm) will apply.

HANDICAPS

The Rules of Golf do not legislate for the allocation and adjustment of handicaps or their playing differentials. Such matters are within the jurisdiction and control of the National Union concerned and queries should be directed accordingly.

CLUBS

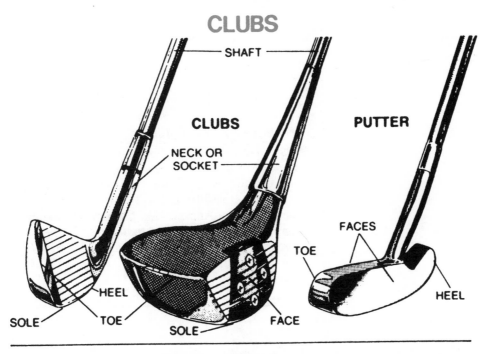

CLUBS

SHAFT

NECK OR SOCKET

HEEL

SOLE

TOE

PUTTER

FACES

TOE

HEEL

SOLE

FACE

GRIPS

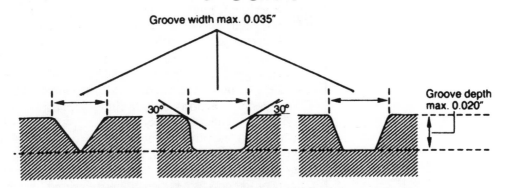

CLUB GRIP CIRCULAR

PUTTER GRIP FLAT SIDE (Permitted on Putters only)

GROOVES

Groove width max. 0.035"

30°   30°

Groove depth max. 0.020"

EXAMPLES OF PERMISSIBLE GROOVE CROSS-SECTIONS

RULES OF AMATEUR STATUS

(Effective from 1st January 1987)

As Approved by

The Royal and Ancient Golf Club

of St. Andrews

Definition of an Amateur Golfer

An Amateur Golfer is one who plays the game as a non-remunerative or non-profit-making sport.

The Governing Body

The Governing Body of golf for the Rules of Amateur Status in any country is the National Union of the country concerned except in Great Britain and Ireland where the Governing Body is the Royal and Ancient Golf Club of St. Andrews.

Any person who considers that any action he is proposing to take might endanger his Amateur Status should submit particulars to the appropriate Committee of the Governing Body for consideration.

RULE 1

Forfeiture of Amateur Status at any age

The following are examples of acts which are contrary to the Definition of an Amateur Golfer and cause forfeiture of Amateur Status:

1. Professionalism.

a. Receiving payment or compensation for serving as a Professional golfer or a teaching or playing assistant to a Professional golfer.

b. Taking any action for the purpose of becoming a Professional golfer except applying unsuccessfully for the position of a teaching or playing assistant to a Professional golfer.

Note 1: Such actions include filing application to a school or competition conducted to qualify persons to play as Professionals in tournaments; receiving services from or entering into an agreement, written or oral, with a sponsor or professional agent; agreement to accept payment or compensation for allowing one's name or likeness as a skilled golfer to be used for any commercial purpose; and holding or retaining membership in any organisation of Professional golfers.

Note 2: Receiving payment or compensation as a shop assistant is not itself a breach of the Rules, provided duties do not include playing or giving instruction.

2. Playing for Prize Money.

Playing for Prize money or its equivalent in a match, tournament or exhibition.

3. Instruction.

Receiving payment or compensation for giving instruction in playing golf, either orally, in writing, by pictures or by other demonstrations, to either individuals or groups.

Exceptions:

1. Golf instruction may be given by an employee of an educational institution or system to students of the institution or system and by camp counsellors to those in their charge, provided that the total time devoted to golf instruction during a year comprises less than 50 percent of the time spent during the year in the performance of all duties as such employee or counsellor.

2. Payment or compensation may be accepted for instruction in writing, provided one's ability or reputation as a golfer was not a major factor in his employment or in the commission or sale of his work.

4. Prizes and Testimonials.

(a) Acceptance of a prize or prize voucher of retail value exceeding as follows:

	In GB & I	Elsewhere
For an event of more than 2 rounds	£170	$400 US or the equivalent
For an event of 2 rounds or less	£110	$260 US or the equivalent

or such lesser figure, if any, as may be decided by the Governing Body of golf in any country, or

(b) Acceptance of a testimonial in Great Britain and Ireland of retail value exceeding £170, elsewhere of retail value exceeding $400 US or the equivalent, or such lesser figure as may be decided by the Governing Body of golf in any country, or

(c) For a junior golfer, of such age as may be determined by the Governing Body of golf in any country, taking part in an event limited exclusively to juniors, acceptance of a prize or prize voucher in Great Britain and Ireland of retail value exceeding £50; elsewhere of retail value exceeding $120 or the equivalent, or such lesser figure, if any, as may be decided by the Governing Body of golf in any country, or

(d) Conversion of a prize or prize voucher into money, or

(e) Accepting a gratuity in connection with a golfing event

Exceptions:

1. Prizes of only symbolic value, provided that their symbolic nature is distinguished by distinctive permanent marking.

2. More than one testimonial award may be accepted from different donors even though their total retail value exceeds £170 or $400 U.S., provided they are not presented so as to evade such value limit for a single award.

Note 1. Events covered. The limits referred to in Clauses (a) or (c) above apply to total prize or prize vouchers received by any one person for any event or series of events in any one tournament or exhibition, including hole-in-one or other events in which golf skill is a factor.

Note 1. "Retail value" is the price at which merchandise is available to anyone at a retail source, and the onus of proving the value of a particular prize rests with the donor.

continued

Note 3. Purpose of prize vouchers. A prize voucher may be issued and redeemed only by the Committee in charge of a competition for the purchase of goods from a Professional's shop or other retail source, which may be specified by the Committee. It may not be used for such items as travel or hotel expenses, a bar bill, or a Club subscription.

Note 4. Maximum Value of Prizes in any event for individuals. It is recommended that the total value of scratch or each division of handicap prizes should not exceed twice the maximum retail value of prize permitted in Rule 1-4(a) and (c) in an 18-hole competition, three times in a 36-hole competition, four times in a 54-hole competition and five times in a 72-hole competition.

Note 5. Testimonial Awards. Such awards relate to notable performances or contributions to golf as distinguished from tournament prizes.

5. Lending Name or Likeness.

Because of golf skill or golf reputation receiving or contracting to receive payment, compensation or personal benefit, directly or indirectly, for allowing one's name or likeness to be used in any way for the advertisement or sale of anything, whether or not used in or appertaining to golf except as a golf author or broadcaster as permitted by Rule 1-7.

Note. A player may accept equipment from anyone dealing in such equipment provided no advertisement is involved.

6. Personal Appearance.

Because of golf skill or golf reputation, receiving payment or compensation, directly or indirectly, for a personal appearance.

Exception.

Actual expenses in connection with personal appearances may be paid or reimbursed provided no golf competition or exhibition is involved.

7. Broadcasting and Writing.

Because of golf skill or golf reputation, receiving payment or compensation, directly or indirectly, for broadcasting concerning golf, a golf event or golf events, writing golf articles or books, or allowing one's name to be advertised or published as the author of golf articles or books of which he is not actually the author.

Exceptions:

1. Broadcasting or writing as part of one's primary occupation, or career, provided instruction in playing golf is not included (Rule 1-3).

2. Part-time broadcasting or writing, provided (a) the player is actually the author of the commentary, articles or books, (b) instruction in playing golf is not included and (c) the payment or compensation does not have the purpose or effect, directly or indirectly, of financing participation in a golf competition or golf competitions.

8. Expenses.

Accepting expenses, in money or otherwise, from any source to engage in golf competition or exhibition.

Exceptions:

A player may receive expenses, not exceeding the actual expenses incurred, as follows:

1. From a member of the family or legal guardian;

or

2. As a player in a golf competition or exhibition limited exclusively to players who have not reached their 18th birthday;

or

3. As a representative of his Country, County, Club or similar body in team competitions or team training camps at home or abroad, or as a representative of his Country taking part in a National Championship abroad immediately preceding or following directly upon an international team competition, where such expenses are paid by the body he represents, or by the body controlling golf in the territory he is visiting;

or

4. As an individual nominated by a National or County Union or a Club to engage in an event at home or abroad provided that:

(a)   The player nominated has not reached such age as may be determined by the Governing Body of Golf in the country from which the nomination is made.

(b)   The expenses shall be paid only by the National Union or County Union responsible in the area from which the nomination is made and shall be limited to twenty competitive days in any one calendar year. The expenses are deemed to incude reasonable travelling time and practice days in connection with the twenty competitive days.

(c)   Where the event is to take place abroad, the approval of the National Union of the country in which the event is to be staged and, if the nominating body is not the National Union of the country from which the nomination is made, the approval of the National Union shall first be obtained by the nominating body.

(d)   Where the event is to take place at home, and where the nomination is made by a County Union or Club, the approval of the National Union or the County Union in the area in which the event is to be staged shall first be obtained.

(*Note.* The term "County Union" covers any Province, State or equivalent Union or Association);

or

5. As a player invited for reasons unrelated to golf skill, e.g. celebrities, business associates, etc. to take part in golfing events;

or

6. As a player in an exhibition in aid of a recognised Charity provided the exhibition is not run in connection with another golfing event.

or

7. As a player in a handicap individual or handicap team sponsored golfing event where expenses are paid by the sponsor on behalf of the player to take part in the event provided the event has been approved as follows:

(a)   where the event is to take place at home the approval of the Governing Body (see Definition) shall first be obtained in advance by the sponsor, and

(b)   where the event is to take place both at home and abroad the approval of the two or more Governing Bodies shall first be obtained in advance by the sponsor. The application for this approval should be sent to the Governing Body of golf in the country where the competition commences.

(c)   where the event is to take place abroad the approval of two or more Governing Bodies shall first be obtained by the sponsor. The application for this approval should be sent to the Governing Body of golf in the country whose players shall be taking part in the event abroad.

(*Note 1:* Business Expenses. It is permissible to play in a golf competition while on a business trip with expenses paid provided that the golf part of the expenses is borne personally and is not charged to business. Further, the business involved must be actual and substantial, and not merely a subterfuge for legitimising expenses when the primary purpose is a golf competition.)

(*Note 2:* Private Transport. Acceptance of private transport furnished or arranged for by a tournament sponsor, directly or indirectly, as an inducement for a player to engage in a golf competition or exhibition shall be considered accepting expenses under Rule 1-8.)

9. Scholarships.

Because of golf skill or golf reputation, accepting the benefits of a scholarship or grant-in-aid other than one whose terms and conditions have been approved by the Amateur Status Committee of the Royal and Ancient Golf Club of St. Andrews.

10. Membership.

Because of golf skill accepting membership in a Golf Club without full payment for the class of membership for the purpose of playing for that Club.

11. Conduct Detrimental to Golf.

Any conduct, including activities in connection with golf gambling, which is considered detrimental to the best interests of the game.

RULE 2

Procedure for Enforcement

and Reinstatement

1. Decision on a Breach. Whenever information of a possible act contrary to the Definition of an Amateur Golfer by a player claiming to be an Amateur shall come to the attention of the appropriate Committee of the Governing Body, the Committee, after such investigation as it may deem desirable, shall decide whether a breach has occurred. Each case shall be considered on its merits. The decision of the Committee shall be final.

2. Enforcement. Upon a decision that a player has acted contrary to the Definition of an Amateur Golfer, the Committee may declare the Amateur Status of the player forfeited or require the player to refrain or desist from specified actions as a condition of retaining his Amateur Status.

The Committee shall use its best endeavours to ensure that the player is notified and may notify any interested Golf Association of any action taken under this paragraph.

3. Reinstatement. The Committee shall have sole power to reinstate a player to Amateur Status or to deny reinstatement. Each application for reinstatement shall be decided on its merits. In considering an application for reinstatement, the Committee shall normally be guided by the following principles:

a. Awaiting Reinstatement.

The professional holds an advantage over the Amateur by reason of having devoted himself to the game as his profession; other persons infringing the Rules of Amateur Status also obtain advantages not available to the Amateur. They do not necessarily lose such advantage merely by deciding to cease infringing the Rules. Therefore, an applicant for reinstatement to Amateur Status shall undergo a period awaiting reinstatement as prescribed by the Committee.

The period awaiting reinstatement shall start from the date of the player's last breach of the Definition of an Amateur Golfer unless the Committee decides that it shall start from the date when the player's last breach became known to the Committee.

b. Period Awaiting Reinstatement.

The period awaiting reinstatement shall normally be related to the period the player was in breach. However, no applicant shall normally be eligible for reinstatement until he has conducted himself in accordance with the Definition of an Amateur Golfer for a period of at least two consecutive years. The Committee, however, reserves the right to extend or to shorten such a period. A longer period will normally be required of applicants who have been in breach for more than five years. Players of national prominence who have been in breach for more than five years shall not normally be eligible for reinstatement.

c. One Reinstatement.

A player shall not normally be reinstated more than once.

d. Status While Awaiting Reinstatement.

During the period awaiting reinstatement an applicant for reinstatement shall conform with the Definition of an Amateur Golfer.

He shall not be eligible to enter competitions as an Amateur. He may, however, enter competitions, and win a prize, solely among members of a Club of which he is a member, subject to the approval of his Club; but he may not represent such Club against other Clubs.

Forms of Application for Countries under the Jurisdiction of the Royal and Ancient Golf Club

(a) Each application for reinstatement shall be submitted on the approved form to the County Union where the applicant wishes to play as an Amateur. Such Union shall, after making all necessary enquiries, forward it through the National Union (and in the case of lady applicants, the Ladies' Golf Union) and the appropriate Professional Golfers' Association, with comments endorsed thereon, to the Governing Body of golf in that country. Forms of application for reinstatement may be obtained from the Royal and Ancient Golf Club or from the National or County Unions. The application shall include such information as the Royal and Ancient Golf Club may require from time to time and it shall be signed and certified by the applicant.

(b) Any application made in countries under the jurisdiction of the Royal and Ancient Golf Club of St. Andrews which the Governing Body of golf in that country considers to be doubtful or not to be covered by the above regulations may be submitted to the Royal and Ancient Golf Club of St. Andrews whose decision shall be final.

R. & A. POLICY ON GAMBLING

The Definition of an Amateur Golfer provides that an Amateur golfer is one who plays the game as a non-remunerative or non-profit-making sport. When gambling motives are introduced, evils can arise which threaten the integrity both of the game and of the individual players.

The R&A does not object to participation in wagering among individual golfers or teams of golfers when participation in the wagering is limited to the players, the players may only wager on themselves or their teams, the sole source of all money won by players is advanced by the players and the primary purpose is the playing of the game for enjoyment.

The distinction between playing for prize money and gambling is essential to the validity of the Rules of Amateur Status. The following constitute golf wagering and not playing for prize money:

1. Participation in wagering among individual golfers.
2. Participation in wagering among teams.

Organised Amateur events open to the general golfing public and designed and promoted to create cash prizes are not approved by the R&A. Golfers participating in such events without irrevocably waiving their right to cash prizes are deemed by the R&A to be playing for prize money.

The R&A is opposed to and urges Unions and Clubs and all other sponsors of golf competitions to prohibit types of gambling such as: Calcuttas, auction sweepstakes and any other forms of gambling organised for general participation or permitting participants to bet on someone other than themselves or their teams.

Attention is drawn to Rule 1-11 relating to conduct detrimental to the game, under which players can forfeit their Amateur Status. It is the Club which, by permitting competitions where excessive gambling is involved, or illegal prizes are offered, bears the responsibility for which the individual is penalised, and Unions have the power to invoke severe sanctions against a Club or individual for consistently ignoring this policy.

Help in the Interpretation of the Rules of Golf

Do you know that:

— a player may change clubs after the first 18 holes of a 36 hole match (4-4a/8).

— if a player searches for a lost ball for ten minutes, he is subject to penalty for undue delay (6-7/2).

— a player may ask the length of a hole (8-1/1) or the distance from a permanent object, e.g. tree, bunker, etc. to the putting green (8-1/2). This is not 'advice'. However, a player may not ask the distance from a non-permanent object, e.g. his ball, to the putting green (8-1/4).

— a player may break off or pull out grass growing behind a ball on the teeing ground (13-2/3).

— a player may play a left-handed stroke with the back of the head of a right-handed club, provided the ball is fairly struck at and the club conforms with the Rules (14-1/1).

— a player may leave the flagstick as he finds it or have it centred in the hole. The player may not adjust the flagstick to a more favourable position than centred. (17/4).

— If after a player has replaced his ball on the putting green and the ball is at rest, a sudden gust of wind then blows the ball into a new position, the player must play the ball from the new position, because wind is not an outside agency (18-1/2).

— a player, whose ball is found within the five minute period, may abandon another ball that has been teed, but not another ball that has been dropped as this ball is in play under Rule 20-4 (27-1/1 and 27-1/2).

A Third Edition of "Help..." was issued in January 1988 to coincide with the introduction of the revised Rules of Golf.

The Third Edition refers to over 350 of the Decisions contained in the Joint Decisions Book of the Royal and Ancient Golf Club of St. Andrews and the United States Golf Association.

It should be required reading for all officials and players will find it an excellent means of improving their knowledge and understanding of the Rules.

PRICE (Including postage and packing).

G.B. & I – £4.00 Rest of Europe – £4.50; Rest of World – £6.00

Available from the Royal and Ancient Golf Club of St. Andrews, Fife KY16 9JD.

DECISIONS ON THE RULES OF GOLF

**by the
Royal and Ancient Golf Club of St. Andrews
and the United States Golf Associaiton**

RULES REVISION

In 1984 The Royal and Ancient Golf Club of St. Andrews and the United States Golf Association put into effect the first comprehensive revision of the Rules of Golf since international uniformity (other than the specifications of the ball) was achieved in 1952.

UNIFORM DECISION WORLD-WIDE

The R & A and the USGA took advantage of this oportunity to achieve uniformity of interpretation of the Rules by combining their two Decision Services into a single completely rewritten Decisions Service for world-wide reference.

ESSENTIAL REFERENCE BOOK FOR ALL COMPETITION ORGANISERS AND CLUB COMMITTEES

The Decisions are now available in one compact readily portable book. The book contains almost 1,000 Decisions which will assist a Committee in resolving many of the everyday problems, as well as the more unusual ones, which arise at all levels of competitive golf.

REGULAR UPDATING OF DECISIONS

A complete new book will be available each year. It will include any new Decision and those which have been revised in the course of the year.

*Apply to Secretary, Royal and Ancient Golf Club
of St. Andrews, Fife KY16 9JD*

Printed by McNaughtan & Sinclair Ltd. Glasgow.